Clematis Nelly Moser.

A well established terrace in traditional style.

The ABC of Patio and Terrace Gardening

Even non-gardeners must envy the comfort, beauty, and privacy provided by a shady patio aglow with vibrant colour. To sit amid the plants, sipping a drink and with a favourite book in hand, or maybe just dreaming whilst the bees go about their business, is for many gardeners just a dream.

To plant a successful patio garden with year-round interest is not easy, but with the right advice it is possible. Here is a colourful and informative book based on years of practical experience that shows how a beautiful patio can be created, providing year-round colour, privacy, and easy maintenance. The right choice of plants that will thrive in the prevailing conditions is essential and is often learned at considerable expense. Following Gay Nightingale's advice, these frustrating and expensive mistakes can be avoided. Many alternative plants for differing situations are suggested so that you can create a unique patio that reflects your own personal choice and provides your own secluded retreat from the rigours of everyday life.

ABC of

Patio and Terrace Gardening

Gay Nightingale

A small new patio in a town garden.

John Bartholomew and Son Limited
London and Edinburgh

First Published in Great Britain 1977
by John Bartholomew and Son Limited
216 High Street, Bromley BR1 1PW and at
12 Duncan Street, Edinburgh EH9 1TA

ISBN 0 7028 1093 2

Printed in Great Britain

CONTENTS

ABC of Patio & Terrace Gardening

Acknowledgements
The author would like to acknowledge with grateful thanks the kind encouragement and help received from Mr. A. Hamid, and Dr. A. K. Wells during the preparation of this book.

Picture Credits
Half Title and Title page, Harry Smith
Colour photographs: *Viola* Jesse East, p.52; Lilium Brandywise, p.64, *Jasminum nudiflorum*, p.52 are by Dr. A. K. Wells, Tomato Pixie with Whirlybird nasturtium, p.52 and *Sempervivum*, p.49 are by the author. All other photographs provided by Iris Hardwick Horticultural Collection.

A modern brick terrace whose large area is broken by the careful placing of planters.

Introduction

What is a patio?

The use of the word has become confused over the last few years. Indeed, I would go so far as to say that it has taken on a new meaning.

Originally, it was a Spanish word for a courtyard built into the centre of a house, protected from view on all sides by walls—an opening in the centre of the home, where members of the family could relax amid greenery without being seen.

These patches of light, air, and paving, were inspired copies taken from Persian Gardens, and adapted to suit Spanish environments by the invading Arabs in the eighth century A.D.

The Arabs appreciated seclusion and shady interiors which were open to the sky. The provision of cooling water in quiet pools was considered an extra delight, probably because of the strong contrast to the parched deserts of Arabia.

Today, a patio is still regarded as an enclosed, or partly enclosed area of the house, whilst any raised paved area adjacent to the house is considered to be a terrace. Pillars and ballustrades are sometimes incorporated in the design.

The *modern* meaning of the word 'patio' can encompass either an enclosed area, an exposed area; a straight or circular strip of paving—either attached to the house on one side, or detached; either sheltered by walls, or unsheltered. It is often used in place of the word 'terrace.'

Most patios or terraces are paved, or else the ground is covered with cobbles, bricks, tiles or terrazzo. These materials can be used separately or in combinations to achieve various effects.

In this book, I have stretched the meaning even further, to include a small yard, perhaps laid with concrete or crazy paving, where it is intended that plants should grow in pots and tubs, or containers of any description.

What is patio gardening?

Simply, an exciting aspect of horticulture—but perhaps this is not easy to see all at once. Before it is possible to visualize the scope of gardening in any sphere it is necessary to know the limitations of your particular site.

Patios are built not only in all sorts of shapes and sizes, but they are made to serve so many separate purposes. Here are some examples—taken at random:

1. Plain paving with perhaps a solitary tub.
2. Paving broken by a ring of beds—believe it or not, glass cloches have been seen propped along the lines like miniature greenhouses—full of lettuces!
3. Paving surrounded by raised beds bordered by low brick walls.
4. Terrace rockeries beside shallow steps.
5. A paved area used as a background to plants in pots, hanging baskets and window boxes.
6. A pool garden set in tiles with pergola and climbing plants.

Obviously, a wider selection of gardening activities could take place on some patios than on others. But the smallest space can be made interesting by a careful choice of rare or otherwise intriguing plants. Not forgetting that flowers and foliage may also be chosen purely for their colour and form.

To me, the pattern a plant makes on stone or brick is inspiring. In this way, gardening against paving becomes more than just plants and stone—the scene changes with the seasons in a kaleidoscopic re-arrangement, as petals drop, and leaves turn through all the greens to red and gold. The design may be improved by adding or subtracting extraordinary specimens.

Remember, too, the sculptural smoothness of terra cotta pots and urns, and the decorative effect of a statue as a centre point.

Gardening knowledge is helpful when it comes to the selection of plants—species, varieties and hybrids; and in the understanding of which particular plants do well in individual situations: better results are bound to be obtained where a plant is sited to obtain optimum growing conditions.

The A–Z section will give some idea of the range and variety of plants which can be grown in a number of different ways in all kinds of patios.

The advantages of a patio or terrace

They are many. But I would place them in this order:

1. Seclusion can be arranged in a short time on a patio with screening, trellis, fences, walling or plants.
2. The paving—if it adjoins the house—provides a platform which is architecturally pleasing in that it seems to settle the house into its surroundings.
3. On wet days or during a muddy winter, gardening work can be continued in comparative comfort.
4. Heavy digging—even in patio beds—is not necessary.
5. Weeding becomes such an easy job, that in these circumstances, it can be described as a pleasant occupation.
6. Raised beds, pots, baskets, tubs, urns, boxes, reduce backbending to a minimum.
7. It is easier to protect precious plants from children, cats, dogs, insects and weather, than when they are in the open garden.
8. Screening provides protection from strong winds for both plants and for people.

Containers can be changed around. This need not be only for decorative purposes. Some exotic plants require cover during the winter; and pots may be moved in and out of the house or greenhouse, according to the season.

Part One

Learning from experience

The only way to learn about gardening is from practical experience or by reading the advice of others. Books help in that they suggest plants and methods that have been tested and tried in various growing mediums; and may inspire you to experiment with unusual plants, or unusual groupings. Papers and magazines are also a great help and enable you to keep in touch with the latest results being produced by other gardeners.

Then there is the experience that is gained every time you potter around yourself: sowing seeds, pricking out seedlings, noticing the results of various compost mixtures, and the water requirements of delicate specimens.

There is much to be said for joining a horticultural society, as it is stimulating to swop stories and experiences, and much useful knowledge can be gained in this way. Most local societies always try to encourage new members.

Practical, first-hand experience is important as some of your own experiments may prove to be unique. New ideas which you try yourself may lead you to discover a useful display method, or a new or more productive technique in seed sowing, or raising. Sometimes the best things we learn from experience happen by mistake.

For example, some years ago, I had sown several clay pans of hardy cyclamen seed. After exposure to frost for a week or two, the pans were placed in a greenhouse for germination. Cyclamen seeds are strange in the way they germinate. It can happen after weeks or years. Sometimes frost followed by warmth will bring about the desired effect—sometimes it won't!

Cyclamen coum seed has been known to germinate the first autumn it is sown—especially when fresh seed is used; but it has also been known to germinate five years after sowing. The seeds that I sowed were *Cyclamen neapolitanum* seeds and although I waited and waited for germination, nothing happened! Then after five or six weeks, by chance I noticed some tiny cyclamen leaves on the floor of the greenhouse, against the side where it was shady and damp. I scooped them up and potted them straight away. But not before the natural requirements had been noted. The seeds hadn't germinated in the sandy compost, but they had germinated in the damp, peaty soil, in shade. Don't ask me how the seeds got on to the floor. It must have been a mistake. But the important point is that, since then I have had no trouble with cyclamen seeds. They need humus and moist, shady conditions, plus sufficient drainage material. In fact, I find the easiest place to germinate these tricky seeds is in the parent pots around the edge of the containers away from the parent tuber. And they germinate readily out of doors.

Growing plants from seed

No matter how tiny your paved area, try to find the space to raize a few of your own seedlings. The excitement of waiting for the first flowers entirely makes up for the effort involved.

Of course it is preferable if rather mundane jobs can be carried out in another part of the garden—only bringing plants on to the patio or terrace when they are about to flower, or in the case of foliage plants, when they are growing rapidly and producing healthy leaves in profusion.

But if space outside is limited to the paved or concreted area, then, in my view, it is still worth attempting at least one tray of seeds—and in this case, choose a really interesting plant.

Maybe, you will wonder what I suggest as 'a really interesting plant'; and, here, I am afraid I am not going to be as helpful as I wish to be. You see, it depends so much on your own particular likes and dislikes. But if you fancy mainly bright colours, then I can say that for an extremely small space, select a packet of *mixed* varieties, so that at least you will have the pleasure of watching buds develop and wondering what the exact shade or tint will be as the petals open.

Pansies are perfect for all-year colour. And there are special summer-flowering or winter-flowering varieties. Other seeds which have given me a tremendous amount of pleasure over the years, and which I can whole-heartedly recommend for small spaces include: geraniums, dwarf dianthus, pinks and violas.

My main enjoyment comes from trying to raise the flower colour or pattern which I consider would be in some way excellent for patio display. And these plants adapt well to my purpose.

Polyanthus are worth growing at home for the same reasons—lots of colour combinations are possible from the hybrids. Coleus may be chosen if patterned foliage is preferred. Or the patterned foliage of some pelargoniums is fascinating. But in this latter case, you must begin with home-saved seed, as at the time of writing, seed is not sold for patterned foliage varieties of pelargonium. They do not come true to variety. In other words, if you sow your own seed, collected from a plant with brightly patterned foliage, you may get one patterned plant in the off-spring—all the other seedlings may be plain. However, there are great opportunities here for the person who enjoys an intriguing hobby. Any gardener could raise an exciting new variety of pelargonium with patterned foliage. And if you begin with the miniatures they need not take much space.

Your own personal delights might take you in another direction—towards alpines or bulbs for example, and a seed-sowing programme can be arranged around your requirements.

If you are lucky enough to have a really large patio or several terraces, you may decide to dabble in more than one direction. Trying different kinds of plants is one of the best ways of finding out what appeals to you.

When choosing plants to grow from seed—even if you are looking for mixed-colour varieties—always try to obtain the best strains and cultivars available. It is worth paying a little extra for good seed. A lot of care will have gone into the breeding of the parent plants; the colours will be brighter, and the pattern of the petals or foliage more distinct.

It is also exciting raising a rare plant from seed—something a little unusual—something that isn't growing in every other house or garden in the road. There are rare alpines and rare bulbs which you can grow at home from seed quite easily. There are rare species of almost every genus. The main problem is usually the availability of the seed in the first place. But some nurseries specialize in rare plants.

Recently, we grew the so-called rare blue amaryllis seed, which came from the Organ Mountains of Brazil. And it was an enthralling process. Even the seeds were an odd size and shape—large, half-moon, and leathery like sea-weed.

Germination wasn't difficult, and the growing bulbs turned out to be less tender than expected. Eventually, each bulb is supposed to grow as big as a foot-ball! And the flowers—blue trumpets—have rarely been seen. There is something romantic about the blue colour, trumpets, and Organ Mountains. But even I was surprised at the correspondence which the subject attracted, when I mentioned the seeds in a newspaper column.

The point about growing rare plants is that they are individually interesting. If you are growing a well-known variety you will probably have seen the flowers before, and part of the thrill of waiting for the first burst of colour as the buds begin to unfold will be missing.

Planning a plant cross

Obviously, on a compact, paved area we should not contemplate a large-scale plant breeding programme, such as would be carried out commercially in order to produce a new kind of bloom or foliage pattern. But it is an absorbing occupation even when attempted on a minute scale.

Commercially, or in a private garden of several acres, parent plants might be chosen for a near-perfect form, or for a striking colour, or for a new outline, and labelled accordingly. Little notes would be made in gardening diaries, so that an exact record would be in existence of every success—and every failure—and more important, the successes could be repeated if necessary.

The whole operation would be under control—right to the point of removing the stamens or anthers of a flower that is to be cross-fertilized by the pollen from the anthers of another flower. The female part of the flower, the stigma, would be protected to prevent bees or other insects from performing the fertilization ceremony!

You *can* go into this amount of detail on a patio; but it is more usual to potter about happily removing the seeds from a flower which you particularly like, and sowing them to see what happens. If a better flower than the parent develops from a batch of seedlings, then save the seeds from that specimen and so on. It's a lovely pastime—if a little haphazard!

The procedure can be more complicated than this. Certainly, it should be noted that plant-cross results with wide variety in the off-spring are more likely to come from hybrid parents. The arrangement of characteristics will vary according to the laws of genetics, and there is more of a pattern in this than first meets the eye. Plant breeders sometimes work out their results on paper before they begin. It is a fascinating subject.

One most important rule, which concerns patio gardening, is the fact that pure-bred plants with a Latin species name will probably breed true to their type—that is, all the seedlings will grow up to look the same as the parent. But this may not be the case, if another similar species or variety is growing close by, as a natural cross might occur.

Preparing the seed tray

First wash the tray if it is new. It is also a good idea to get into the habit of scrubbing out all seed trays at the end of the season. Dirty trays might keep pests and diseases going from one year to the next. Some gardeners like to spread a layer of broken crocks or flower-pot chippings at the base of the trays. I do this myself if I am using a John Innes type of compost; but with the modern, peaty composts it is unnecessary. There is no need to press the compost into the trays, as this will only push out the air. If the soil is not already quite moist give it a good watering with a fine 'rose' on the watering-can.

Sowing the seed

Next comes the important stage of actually planting the seed. The main mistake, here, I think, can be sowing too thickly—it makes twice the work when pricking out the seedlings later. Try to leave a gap between each seed and the next, although this is not always easy, and sometimes impossible with fine seed. Cover very carefully with compost—no deeper than the depth of the seed itself.

The stage which is often omitted in seed sowing technique is the last one. A sheet of glass is placed over the tray to stop some of the water from evaporating too quickly, and drying out the seed-coats. Finally, a piece of paper goes on top of the glass, until the seed leaves begin to show. The glass-and-paper technique is not absolutely essential, but it does seem to aid the germination process in many cases, since a dry seed-coat causes difficulties when the tender seed leaves try to unfold. Hard skin can sometimes prevent this happening altogether. If the compost is allowed to become bone dry for any length of time the young seedlings will be completely lost, so care must be taken to avoid drying out.

Plastic seed trays may be used for some types of seed; clay pans for others. The plastic containers should last for years so long as you do not lift a full tray by one end, as this could cause the side to crack. Clay pans do not break easily unless they are accidentally dropped, or knocked against each other.

Seed composts

1. Sandy soil mixtures. These are suitable for alpines; cacti and succulents; some herbaceous plants.

2. John Innes Compost (soil mixture) To make this up for yourself, you mix two buckets of horticultural loam (grass turf which has been stacked and rotted down) one bucket of horticultural sand (with no sea salt) and one bucket of peat. Then add one and a half ounces of superphosphate, and three quarters of an ounce of ground chalk per bushel of the above mixture. Leave out the chalk for camellias, and other lime-hating plants.

3. Peat-based mixtures. These composts are sometimes referred to as soil-less mixtures. It is usually the loam that is missing, as it is difficult to obtain in some countries.

Types of germination

Because seeds come in many forms, they can be very small; large with a hard seed coat; or the embryo may be embedded in a carbohydrate substance; they take varying lengths of time to germinate and require individual environmental conditions.

Some seeds will germinate in a matter of hours. Morning glory (*Ipomoea*) has been seen to let the butterfly-shaped seed-leaves emerge from the seed-coat over night. A cyclamen on the other hand, can take several years before releasing a solitary seed-leaf from a seed; while the normal germination time for many annuals and perennials is between one and two weeks—sometimes up to four.

The right external conditions are important if seeds are to be stimulated into beginning the germination process; the essentials are heat, light, water and air. Different seeds vary considerably in their requirements. Some need very warm soil conditions and others a period of freezing conditions followed by warmth. The time of year during which the seed is planted also affects the process.

Hard seeds may germinate more quickly if the seed-coat is chipped gently. But this is not so easy as it sounds as seeds tend to be difficult to hold. If you soak large specimens such as sweet peas, lupins, or broom, before attempting to chip, you should have more success.

Some shrubs, certain species of hardy cyclamen and other alpines, which need a period of cold to break their dormancy, are best sown in late summer, but even then patience is needed. Do not throw away the contents of seed trays, if germination does not occur during the first year. You may have a pleasant surprise three or four years later!

A trick or two with temperatures

In cool climates, there is often a great urge to get started with seed sowing early in the season. The idea is to make the most of a limited period when a large number of showy plants flourish out of doors. If you own a heated greenhouse, you can start early as the seedlings will obtain all the light and warmth they should have for natural development.

But there is another way of starting early too. If you have a greenhouse which is not heated, you can sow seeds early indoors. Carry the seedlings out at first light in the mornings and back into the warmth of the house at night. Although this method requires a lot of enthusiasm and energy on the part of the grower, the period when the nights will be too cold for the seedlings to be left out is usually short, perhaps only four weeks or so.

Yet another possibility regarding early starts is to use a large window, conservatory, or glass home extension, with or without the use of one of the excellent propagators which are now on the market. But the point must be made that where it is not easy to provide sufficient heat and light, it is best to wait and make a slightly later start, as less seedlings will be lost when the weather warms up and there is more daylight.

Many seeds need a constant temperature of 60–64°F (15–18°C) during the period of germination; and the seeds of some exotic plants will need an even higher temperature. In these circumstances a propagator is a very useful piece of equipment.

Half-hardy plants can be grown to almost the point of petals opening by the time the weather is warm enough to transfer them to their outside display positions.

There are, of course, some seeds which need no artificial heat, and these may be sown straight into pots out of doors, or even straight into raised flower beds. There are many hardy annuals such as marigolds, nasturtiums, etc., and some hardy perennials are suitable.

Pricking out the seedlings

This can be a pleasant occupation, or it can be a bore, depending on the way the job is done. If you have to bend over it will be back-breaking. Try to place the small seed trays on a raised platform or bench, which is at a convenient height for you. Have boxes or large-size plastic trays to one side. Fill them with fresh John Innes or peaty compost, and proceed to transplant one seedling at a time into its new home.

It is usually time to transplant when the seed-leaves are properly developed, and the next pair, the first pair of true leaves is beginning to form. Seedlings should be spaced well apart, leaving an area around each one for the roots to develop. Sometimes a special forked, two-pronged stick is used to prick the seedlings out of the soil; but any kind of small fork will do. A point worth making here, is that cuttings are usually taken in order to gain replicas of the specimen in hand, while seeds are sown in order to get variety and novelty. Cuttings are taken to increase the stock of any new form that emerges after the seed sowing process. Seed sowing is a sexual method of reproduction: the genes are mixed and re-arranged in different patterns giving rise to new plant characteristics. Rooting cuttings is known as a vegetative method of reproduction: the genes remain in exactly the same pattern as is found in the parent with no new plant characteristics.

The above is an important rule in botany; but it is also a useful phenomenon where gardening is concerned: it is interesting to note how much of horticulture depends on patterns, from the formation of microscopic dots to daring designs in flowers, foliage, and paving stones. Life itself can be seen as a series of kaleidoscopic patterns; and the gardener gains a little knowledge of these patterns, and how to change them, or how to maintain them.

Raising plants from cuttings

When you grow or buy a plant which you like, more plants with identical characteristics can be obtained by vegetative propagation. In many cases, this means taking cuttings. A leaf, or leaf-bud, or short stem with leaves attached is taken from the plant and rooted under special conditions. Different methods are used for different plants. For instance, leaves are more often used in the case of tropical plants, e.g. African violets (*Saintpaulia*); panda plants (*Kalanchoe tomentosa*); some begonias. Leaf-buds are often used with alpines, e.g. *Primula marginata.* Stem cuttings are taken as the most usual method of propagating shrubs and herbaceous plants, also many types of house plants.

Leaf cuttings. Sometimes the whole leaf and petiole (stalk) is used as in African violets, or just the leaf, as in the panda plant. Sometimes a part of a leaf is used as in *Sansevieria.* Sometimes sections of leaf-veins are used as in Rex begonias. African violet leaves will root in water in a warm place; otherwise choose a peaty compost.

Leaf bud cuttings. *Camellia* is a good example. You take a leaf with a bud at the base, and a little of the surrounding wood. Plant so that only the leaf is above the soil surface.

Bud cuttings. In the case of *Primula marginata*, a side-shoot leaf-bud is detached from the parent plant and rooted in a sand-and-peat mixture.

General. Whereas the method of taking cuttings varies from plant to plant (and it is best to look up the individual genus or species before beginning the job), there are a few general rules which apply—not always, but time and time again.

The compost should be 'open', that is, mixed with grit or sand to allow quick drainage; but it also needs to hold sufficient water for the developing roots, and peat is often used for this purpose. It needs to be sterilized, so that soil pests and diseases will not attack young plants before they have a chance to form properly.

It is not necessary to have fertilizer in a medium for rooting cuttings, although some gardeners use a John Innes mixture from the very beginning. Peat-and-sand in equal proportions is preferred in many cases, but some kind of fertilizer will be needed as soon as the roots have formed. At this stage plants may be re-potted into compost in which balanced fertilizers have been incorporated.

A cold frame or unheated greenhouse is invaluable for rooting cuttings, or a propagator as suggested under the seed sowing heading. The propagator is most useful for rooting exotic plants, although it is surprising how many successful results can be obtained on an ordinary window sill. To preserve the moisture content in the buds, leaves, or stems used for propagating, make sure there is some shade during the hottest part of the day. A humid atmosphere is beneficial in many cases.

There is a substance called hormone rooting powder, and although many cuttings will root without this, it can be helpful with subjects that are slow to respond to normal treatment.

Other forms of vegetative propagation

Increasing by root division. *Aspidistra*, *Polyanthus*, many herbaceous plants, and many alpines, can be simply divided at soil level: several single roots with some leaves attached being taken from one large clump; each root should develop into a new plant when dug into fresh compost.

Air-layering and soil-layering. The first method is applied mostly to plants which form new roots on the stem in the air quite naturally, or extremely easily, as seen in the rubber plant (*Ficus*).

To make a new plant, very carefully cut into the stem about 2 in. (5 cm.) below the last leaf. Wrap some sphagnum moss around the stem, holding it in place with a piece of polythene and an easy tie. In a few weeks, the roots will grow into the moss, and the top part of the stem can be removed and planted up in a separate pot. The old, lower stem should form fresh side shoots.

The second method of layering is common in cool climates. Wisteria and jasmine are examples of woody plants which develop new roots along the stem, providing part of it has constant contact with moist soil. This occurs quite naturally, but the process may be encouraged by gardeners who wish to increase their stock. Stems are pegged down and the end which emerges from the soil is supported with a cane. When roots form, the young plant is detached from the old one. The last quarter is the usual time for soil-layering preparations. Patience is necessary as the young plants may take many months to become established; but this method used for propagating rhododendrons is much quicker than rooting cuttings.

Corms and tubers. The thick food storage organs in some plants such as begonias and dahlias can be cut into sections. Each part that retains a growing point, a young shoot or bud, will develop into a new plant.

Other types of plants form new corms or tubers which can be detached from the previous year's growth quite easily without cutting; and these separate units are a simple form of vegetative propagation. Young plants raised in this way may take longer than one year to reach flowering size.

It is worth noting that cyclamen cannot be increased by these vegetative methods, as little corms do not form around the old plants.

Bulbs. Most people know that a group of daffodils will gradually increase in number over the years if left undisturbed. The baby bulbils may be taken away from the parent plant and potted up or planted out on their own. In time every bulbil will reach flowering size.

Potting and re-potting

Anyone who is keen on pots themselves, as well as propagating with their own seeds and cuttings, will quite enjoy the various potting-on stages that become necessary—even if it can seem like hard work, when there are a great number of plants to move at one time.

The enjoyment comes from having raised, say, a rare blue amaryllis bulb from seed, and, having seen it develop so that the roots fill a small pot, speculation brings excitement as to how fast it will grow in a larger size pot with fresh compost.

The same kind of enthusiasm surrounds every stage of gardening on the patio or terrace. I like my pots. They are in themselves a collection. Clay pots of all shapes and sizes have a definite appeal for me. But plastic pots are extremely useful too, and most gardeners gradually accumulate a mixed assortment.

The various inch or centimetre sizes refer to the diameter of the top measurement: 3 in. (7.5 cm.) 4 in. (10 cm.) etc. The term half-pot, which is common in the horticultural world, refers to the depth of the pot, that is, it will be half the height of the ordinary pot. Very useful for alpines and small bulbs, e.g. *Androsace*, species crocus, etc. Pans are shallower still; they are especially suitable for seedlings, and some low-growing alpines, e.g. *Saxifraga*.

The first potting. This usually takes place when seedlings become too big for a seed tray. They are young plants with, perhaps, four leaves and and a half-developed root system. Obviously, every care has to be taken to avoid damaging the tender roots.

The plant can be tipped gently out of its pot and you should find a mat of woven roots inside. This is known as the root-ball. When potting-on this root-ball should be disturbed as little as possible, merely packing fresh compost at the base, and round the sides in a pot only one size larger.

Re-potting. When you reach a certain size pot in the potting-on process, you may decide that you do not want to use a larger size pot. This is likely to happen when the plant has grown into a mature specimen of its kind.

In this case, some of the stale compost is removed without breaking the new roots. The old roots or dead roots can be removed at the same time. Old roots of *Fuchsia*, *Hippeastrum* and some orchids, will actually look as if they need removing, so there should be no trouble in deciding which roots to take and which roots to leave.

The next stage involves working some fresh compost into the new space, putting a little over the top, ensuring that the root-ball does not lie too deep. This is usually done at the end of the resting season. Note that resting seasons vary with different types of plants: i.e. some plants rest in summer, some in winter, etc.

Top dressing. Those plants that are so large that you cannot easily remove them from their pots should have a top dressing of fresh compost.

The old soil is carefully scraped from the top taking care to avoid damage to the roots of the plant, and the space filled with new compost. This has to be done about once a year.

Types of soil

You will often see or hear the expression 'lime-hating plants' meaning that some plants will not grow where there is chalk or lime present in the soil. Examples include: camellias, rhododendrons, heathers, cassiopes. They are also sometimes referred to as acid-loving. They grow best in a soil mixture of sand and humus, or a mixture of peat and sand and humus. But with no lime—even the lime present in tap water of some districts will be harmful to these plants.

The term 'lime-loving' is not often heard; but in fact, there are plants which do well in limestone districts, and numerous plants, for example, *Aubrieta*, *Clematis*, *Dianthus*, flourish in a moderately alkaline soil.

If you have been gardening for some years, you will probably know which of your plants need an acid soil, and which need an alkaline soil. You will also have some idea of your own garden soil.

Hydrangeas are natural indicators of soil alkalinity or acidity as the flowers turn blue or bluish-purple on acid soil, and pink or pinky-mauve on alkaline soil. And of course, any soil mixture can be used in containers, mixed according to a plant's requirements if necessary.

pH scale

This is a means of assessing acidity or alkalinity of the soil by analysis. A simple do-it-yourself kit can be purchased. The chemicals supplied will turn pink or blue, or green for neutral, when mixed with a small sample of soil and the precise result can be compared with the accompanying chart which is marked with numbers corresponding to grades of pink or blue. The neutral green will give a number 7. And we say that pH 7 is neutral. Low numbers will be acid; high numbers alkaline etc.

There is really no need to go to this trouble with container gardening, where you can mix up your own composts; but a knowledge of the pH values of your soil is useful if you are starting a new garden from scratch. By closely observing the weeds that grow vigorously, an intelligent guess at your soil conditions can be made, as certain weeds only grow well on certain types of soil. This is another example of learning by experience. For a list of the indicator plants see under Weeds.

Types of compost

I am often asked 'What is the difference between the various JI Composts?' and 'Why are there different numbers?' or 'Which compost number do I use?'

The answers are simple. The difference between one kind of JI Potting Compost and another is that more or less fertilizer has been added according to the number. For example, JI No. 2 has twice the amount as JI No. 1.

Therefore, we choose the compost which suits the plant we are growing. JI No. 1 is usually selected when we want a soil mixture for pricking out seedlings, or potting up young plants at the four-leaf stage. JI No. 2 is the most likely choice for potting-on plants into larger containers, or for mixed groupings of half-hardy plants such as geraniums, petunias, etc. JI No. 3 is chosen for large plants and some shrubs or fast-growing chrysanthemums, etc.

John Innes Seed Compost (see under seed-sowing).

John Innes Potting Compost No. 1.

7 buckets sterilized loam
3 buckets of peat
2 buckets of sand

It doesn't matter what size the bucket is.

Then mix thoroughly before adding 4 oz John Innes Base per bushel. (Four 2-gallon buckets will hold one bushel altogether.)

Tip out the measured bushel of mixed soil, and mix again with the fertilizers.

John Innes Potting Compost No. 2.

Use the same soil mixture as given above for JI No. 1., but add *twice* the amount of JI Base per bushel.

John Innes Potting Compost No. 3.

Use the same mixture as given for JI No. 1., but add *three* times the amount of JI Base per bushel.

John Innes Base

Ground hoof and horn—2 parts (weight).
Calcium phosphate—2 parts.
Potassium sulphate—1 part.

Note that all these mixtures can be purchased in handy bags from garden shops in some countries. Note also that gardeners tend to develop their own variations on the John Innes mixtures if they have a special interest in any one kind of plant. For instance, if you are a cactus collector, you will want to add more grit—possibly in the form of fine stone chippings. If you are keen on plants which do not grow well where lime is present, say heathers, remember to omit the chalk from any of these composts.

Carnation-lovers tend to favour a loam, sand, manure, and bonfire-ash combination. Cyclamen enthusiasts are concerned with humus and drainage materials such as stone chippings. Orchid growers sell special compost consisting of Osmunda fibre, sphagnum moss, or fir bark and plastic pieces. In addition polystyrene chips are often placed at the bottom of the mixture for drainage.

Every specialist gardener will have his own tips regarding soil mixtures.

Soil-less composts.

These are generally made by mixing one part of peat to one part of sand or grit. The fertilizers are then added to every bushel in the following proportions.

Fertilizer mixture for soil-less composts

Ground hoof and horn	—2 oz
Ammonium nitrate	—½ oz
Potassium sulphate	—1 oz
Magnesian limestone	—2 oz
Chalk	—3 oz
Superphosphate	—2 oz

Feeding of plants

Although people often say 'feed your plants with fertilizers' there is more to plant feeding than the mere addition of fertilizers to the soil. Plants are able to manufacture their own food in a way that humans and animals cannot. It is one of the wonders of life that plants are able to use energy from the sun to synthesise food. This is a process called photosynthesis during which plants take carbon dioxide from the air in daylight, and sugars are built up in the green plant cells. Water is necessary for photosynthesis, as is the green pigment called chlorophyll in the cells. It is this chlorophyll that absorbs the sun's energy. At the end of a complicated chemical chain reaction inside the plant leaves, carbon dioxide and water are turned into sugar and oxygen. These sugars are used, together with elements taken from the water, to build up tissue for separate functions. For example, proteins, fats and vitamins are needed in flowers, fruits, nuts, seeds; essential oils in petals for fragrance; carbohydrates in seed coverings and fibrous tissue.

Plants also need other elements besides carbon, hydrogen and oxygen found in the air and water. It is these which we supply when we put fertilizer into our pot plant compost: nitrogen in a form that the plant can take up from the soil-water is necessary for protein synthesis and leaf development, and general growth; phosphorous is for sturdy stems and a good root system; potassium helps flower formation and the production of starch and sugar. Calcium, magnesium and sulphur are also important. Other elements are required in small quantities. These are known as trace elements and they include iron and manganese.

Some of the elements necessary for the plant's healthy life pass in and out of the leaves via tiny holes (stomata) on the lower surface. This is why waxy or oily substances of any kind will clog the holes and prevent growth.

Be careful when washing leaves. Oils wiped on

to give a fine glossy appearance might kill the plant! Although, some 'leaf shine' sold in bottles is safe so long as it is used according to the maker's instructions.

Fertilizers

There are various fertilizers. But basically they fall into two groups. Those that come from natural, or organic sources, and those that are made from inorganic substances in a laboratory.

The first sort include animal manure, vegetable waste rotted down, garden compost, dried blood, hoof and horn, fish-meal and bone-meal, seaweed.

The second sort includes the chemical fertilizers purchased at garden shops and centres; although some mixtures contain both organic and inorganic substances. Different plants require different fertilizers in balanced proportions. Also, some plants need a little fertilizer while others need a lot.

A brief look at the nitrogen cycle will quickly illustrate how animal remains and excretions return to the plants. It is extremely important to gardeners.

(1) Proteins in animal and plant tissue

(2) Excretion & remains return to soil

(3) They change into ammonia (nitrogen combined with hydrogen)

(4) Nitrogen compounds in soil

(5) Roots of plants

(6) Animals eat plants

This cycle is more complicated than this simple diagram shows, as bacteria and micro-organisms also change the chemical pattern at the various stages, and some of the nitrogen escapes back into the air.

In this modern world we are using more and more chemicals to kill weeds and soil pests. But many of the chemicals which kill the soil pests also kill worms and helpful organisms.

If worms and bacteria are not present in the soil, there is nothing to break down the vegetable and plant remains. Nature's beautifully balanced cycle becomes broken, and the soil becomes infertile or barren. Of course some chemical preparations are necessary, and they do no harm in the right circumstances; but we cannot be too careful about what chemicals we put into our soil—even in pots, boxes, baskets, and garden beds.

It is not simply a matter of whether the chemical will kill me, should I chance to get it on my tongue, or eat a plant recently treated. It is a matter of whether it will kill the worms! Although we don't want worms in our pot plants, the soil in the pots is often returned to the garden quite soon.

I am completely in favour of natural compost gardening, wherever possible. Indeed, if the garden is big enough, and there is a space out of sight, consider making your own compost heap. Most of the kitchen waste of vegetable origin can be saved for compost. It is best if you can put a layer of rabbit, chicken, or other manure between every layer of vegetable and garden waste. But if this is not available place a layer of ordinary garden soil between each layer, and use a sprinkling of a proprietory catalyst to assist in breaking down the waste material.

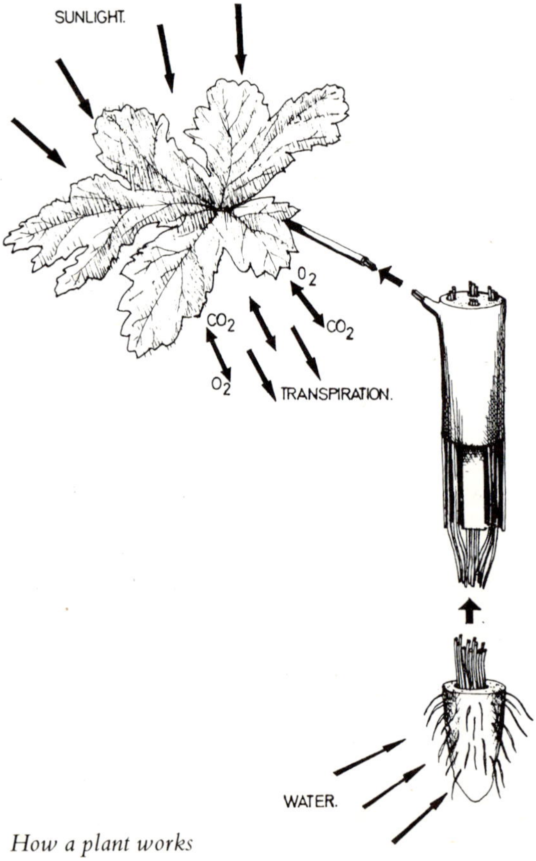

How a plant works

Tablet or pill fertilizers. There are plenty of situations where there is no chance of obtaining well-made natural humus to mix into pot-plant compost. In these circumstances chemical substitutes may be used.

Where plants are kept in the same pots for any length of time over three months, fertilizers may be added to the soil or compost in the pot.

Tablet or pill fertilizers have a long-lasting effect, and good results with flowering pot-plants can be obtained in this way.

Liquid fertilizer. Another way of feeding pot-plants is by using liquid fertilizer, correctly diluted. This works best when given over a long period at regular intervals of ten days to a fortnight during the growing season, and, should never be given to plants in their resting stages.

Feeding through the leaves. Some gardeners like to spray special foliar feeds directly on to the leaves of their pot-plants. I have not found this necessary, as the other ways of providing plant fertilizer have always proved entirely satisfactory for me. However, many people have had splendid results this way.

Sequestrine. It is a good idea to apply this compound to camellias and other lime-hating plants if they show signs of chlorosis—a yellowing of the leaves. This is most likely when they are growing in an alkaline or chalky soil, or when they are given tap-water from a hard-water district.

Watering

It is surprising how many people think that watering plants is simply a matter of filling a can from a tap, and tipping it out over pots, flower beds, etc.

Here are a few of the more important points to keep at the back of your mind next time it's your turn to water the garden!

Amount. Plants in containers of any kind need very frequent watering in summer. This is obvious. But it isn't so often realized that even in winter, plants in pots need watering from time to time—even if they are kept out of doors where rain can reach them. Plants in pots against fences and walls sometimes remain semi-dry in a good down-pour.

There are some plants, for example: geraniums and succulents, which will not die if watering is neglected for a day or two, and it is sensible to choose these if you do not have much time for daily plant-watering routines.

Plants such as ferns and gentians, beautiful though they are, quickly succumb to any dryness at the roots. Others, camellias for example, although they will not actually die if left dry for a day or so, may not flower the following year or their flowering may be reduced.

Temperature. Even hardy plants react badly to very cold water poured straight from the tap on a summer day. And tender plants should always be watered with luke-warm water. It is not only that the temperature of the tap-water is raised to the air-temperature; but much of the chlorine in the water is lost to the atmosphere.

'Hard' water. Where calcium is present in tap-water, this may prove to be too alkaline for 'lime-hating' plants e.g. rhododendrons etc. In this case, rain water should be collected in a can or other container, and used for watering.

Sometimes, a top-dressing of peat around the roots of the plant is helpful where there is no alternative to tap-water. Or, where only a few plants are involved, I have always found cold tea useful! This should be strained, as tea-leaves tend to go mouldy unless they are first made into compost in the usual way.

Direction of spray. Avoid watering over plants with 'hairy' or 'furry' leaves. These are better watered around the dome of foliage, or carefully under the leaves, as the case may be.

Plant pests and diseases

Gardening enthusiasts spend so much time examining their plants that the very first sign of infection or disease is usually detected.

A feeling of horror may grip the gardener when he sees a dreaded sign on a precious plant; but he will be quick in applying the right treatment. And this is one of the secrets of success in gardening: prompt action!

Fungus diseases

1. MILDEW. Most gardeners have heard of mildew on roses. There are several types of this fungus parasite, which can form a powdery substance on stems, leaves, and flower buds. Chrysanthemums and Michaelmas daisies always need watching. Use an anti-mildew spray at the first signs of mould in summer, and repeat a week later.

2. DAMPING OFF. This is a fungus which attacks seedlings, causing them to topple over at compost level. The trouble can be avoided by protecting the seedlings from excessive cold and damp; and also by using sterilized compost.

3. RUST is the common name given to a variety of fungus diseases which develop into tiny dot patterns in browny-orange on the leaves of plants. This is sometimes a nuisance on hollyhocks and pelargoniums (although over the years I have been lucky with the latter!)

4. BOTRYTIS—GREY MOULD attacks plants growing in enclosed places where the air is not freely circulating; and attacks are more common where the temperatures are lower than normally required for healthy growth. Destroy infected plants and improve growing conditions to prevent reoccurrence of the problem.

Virus diseases.

These are difficult to detect. Plants so affected have distorted leaves and stems. If in doubt, send a small specimen away to your local horticultural advisory centre—clearly labelling the sealed container on the outside!

If your specimen turns out to contain a virus, and your suspicions are correct, you will most likely be advised to burn all affected plants and begin again with fresh stock.

Fortunately, viruses do not prevent people from enjoying patio gardening. It is possible to garden for years without worrying about them, or coming across them at all. It seems the natural thing to do to pull up a plant that simply will not respond to treatment of any kind—to do away with it and think no more about it. But do be on the safe side—always burn such a specimen.

Pests

ANTS. I have never really found these much trouble. They do spread greenfly and they do tunnel into the soil in large pots, depriving the roots of shrubs of moisture. But this is the worst—and they are comparatively easy to control.

If you are greatly troubled, special ant-killer preparations can be purchased.

APHIS. Greenfly and blackfly. A real nuisance on some plants, e.g. nasturtiums, cinerarias and sweet peas. But at least they stay almost still. This means they can easily be sprayed as soon as seen.

CATERPILLARS will be seen from time to time in the best-kept garden. Simply pick them off. Sometimes, it is better to take the leaf too—especially if it is nearly all eaten into holes anyway! Most people like butterflies, and remember butterflies mean caterpillars somewhere.

EARWIGS. Another set of hole-makers! You can often catch these fellows in the daytime. They hide in the hollow ends of stems, or in tightly curled young leaves. They seem to have quite a taste for exotic subjects such as daturas, where they make ghastly patterns on the graceful leaves.

Earwigs can be caught in inverted flower pots stuffed with crumpled newspapers and supported on sticks. The paper can be burned at regular intervals.

MEALY BUGS are not much trouble out of doors. But you may come across them on your cacti or succulents. They are flattish, white-grey creatures having little legs all the way round. There is usually a whitish woolly look between the rosettes of foliage, and occasionally one of the animals moves slowly across a leaf. Methylated spirits on a cotton wool swab is the answer, if you can bring yourself to do it. With any luck, you may never see mealy bugs. Just be careful whenever you acquire a new plant. Examine it until you are certain you are not introducing any unwanted strangers to your collection.

RED SPIDER. This tiny mite is just visible, but the web is usually the first sign to catch the gardener's eye. Either this fine web, or the yellow-grey look of the leaves will give the spider away. It is more likely to occur in a greenhouse, conservatory, porch or sunny window, than on an open patio. When seen, spray with a derris solution.

SCALE INSECTS can at times seem like hard brown greenfly. They don't move much, and therefore they are easy to remove with methylated spirit on a soft stick; or spray the plant with a systemic insecticide.

SCIARID MAGGOTS are sometimes seen in pot-plant compost around the roots of plants. They look like ordinary fly maggots only they are smaller, appearing as whitish, short worms with black heads—quite tiny. Kill them by watering the compost with a *very* weak solution of Jeyes fluid; or with malathion.

SLUGS may be caught satisfactorily with half an orange skin. You will be surprised how well this old-fashioned method works. Leave orange peel out over night and remove with the 'catch' every morning.

THRIPS. Again, you may never see this insect. It is about as big as a greenfly, but fast-flying and black in colour. A see-through dot pattern on green leaves is usually a sign of a thrips attack, and if you rustle the leaves, one or two flies may come quickly from their hiding places.

A couple of sprays from a pressure can full of insecticide will clear the plant. Repeat two or three times in successive weeks to prevent more flies hatching out and continuing the life cycle.

White flies are about the same size as thrips, and equally annoying. Spray with insecticide.

Woodlice and worms (See A–Z section). Remember garden worms are *not* pests; but stop them from entering pots through the holes in the base by slipping in a small square of wire gauze at potting time.

Two warnings:

1. Never put chemicals, insecticides, or fungicides in bottles where children can reach them, or even where they might climb up and get them. They could be very dangerous to children who might not read the directions—even if they can read. A responsible, sensible child might chance to use them in the wrong way. All pest-and-disease control chemicals need handling with extreme care even by adults.

2. Don't spray liquids indoors or where people or animals could inhale them. The chemicals may be detrimental to health.

Three helpful suggestions:

1. Well-kept plants may never have any of the above troubles.

2. Scrubbed pots, and sterilized soil will help prevent disease.

3. A handy pressure can will soon clear most of the common pests.

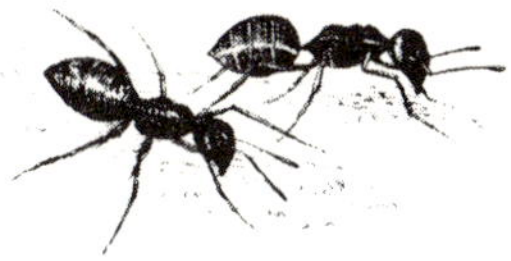

Ant

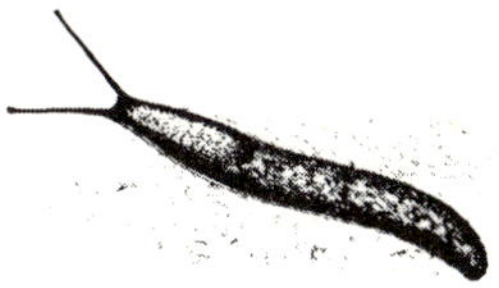

Garden Slug

Aphid

Thrips

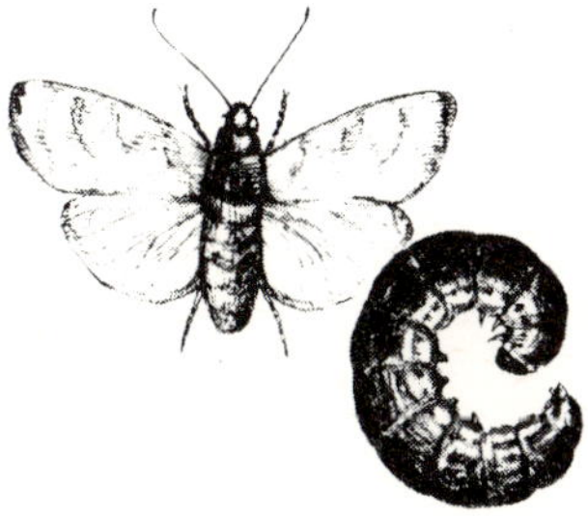

Cutworm

Earwig

Special problems in patio gardening

Briefly, I would say that the common problems of patio or terrace gardening concern space. Usually the lack of it! But in any case, special problems have special solutions. Here are a few of the answers.

Size. If your space is very small, consider paving the whole area. A pot-garden can be satisfying even to the enthusiastic gardener; especially where only the best varieties and species are chosen.

Consider alpine plants, which sometimes look better in pots than they do in the open garden. Make a miniature museum.

If your space is very large, an expanse of paving can be architecturally pleasing. But space can easily be wasted so good design is important. Both pots and plants should be chosen to enhance the overall effect. The solitary sculpture, or Florentine urn may provide an excellent focal point.

Perhaps, foliage will blend around the back with greenery growing tall in beds—the odd blob of a Bourbon rose emerging from the background. To complete the scene, green plants could trail from the urn; and against house walls, large terra cotta pots could carry groups of geraniums. The terrace rockery should take some of the alpines which would be in the tiny pots and pans of the small patio garden.

In large gardens there might be greenhouses or conservatories for tender alpines. Whereas in the smaller garden, some of the choice species of collector's plants which are only just hardy, or not quite hardy, may need a little protection during the coldest months. Prize winning results may be obtained merely by using a sheet of glass, or popping plants into a neat cold frame for the winter.

Creating colour. It is sometimes possible to create a wide variety of colours. Pansies provide an excellent example. One hybrid flower may have all the primary colours in its pansy parentage, and many of the secondary colours may be present too. By taking the ripe seeds from one cross-bred, royal-blue coloured flower, purple and yellow may emerge among the flowers of the seedlings. In the third generation, red flowers may appear, as they did in my own experiment. In this way, a whole patio can be filled with rainbow colour, beginning with only one blue-flowering plant.

When deciding on plants for your terrace you should, whenever practicable, consider the winter scene first. Whatever the size of your garden, plan for winter colour and foliage effect. Greens, golds, browns, from conifers, camellias, heathers, hebes, and alpines of all kinds can be included. Much of the colour from shrubs will stay as a background through the year. Then, against this background, you can place bulbs and other beautiful spring flowering plants; or pelargoniums and petunias in summer. This planned effect may be gained from groups of pots, or container gardening, as well as from raised beds and climbers on walls; and limitations of space or shape seldom prove troublesome if careful thought is given to plant species and their arrangement.

Seclusion makes a garden attractive, and it is essential to the enjoyment of a patio. An enclosed area may be arranged in various ways, one of the simplest being the use of tall-growing shrubs and climbing plants, sometimes set against a background of open-work concrete or trellis.

Choice of plants for seclusion. Quick results are often desired in a new house and garden, and in these circumstances, the following can be recommended for year-round cover in the shortest possible time.

Kerria japonica variety 'pleniflora' for stems which stay dense and green in the winter; a good height—over seven feet; yellow pompon flowers, early in the season before the roses come out; and neat leaves during most of the year.

It is easy to propagate and establish—no trouble with pests—an excellent all-rounder. It even grows and flowers against a north-facing wall.

Broom is a shrub you can grow yourself from seed. It forms a bush of thin branches, and in three or four years, you will have a completely sheltered area, just by raising plants from one packet of seeds. In addition, you will have masses of lupin-like blooms in assorted colours during early summer. In winter, the dark evergreen stems provide a striking contrast to the lighter coloured evergreen stems of kerria. But remember the broom needs a sunnier spot.

Roses. Some climbers and ramblers develop a weave of branches which give a certain amount of seclusion when on a fence support. Golden Showers would be my choice for a yellow flower; Paul's Scarlet for a red flower. The latter grows particularly quickly. These roses have been chosen more for their screening branches than the quality of each individual rose flower, although the blooms *are* attractive in themselves.

Honeysuckle. The healthy shoots of the old *Lonicera japonica* will cover a wire fence or trellis with a thick mat of evergreen foliage, which it is impossible to peep through. And the heavily scented flowers—custard and caramel coloured—which appear all summer even in a shady spot, perfume a whole patio. The scent will waft into the house every time someone enters.

View blocked by buildings. If your out-look is limited to the backs or sides of buildings, it is sometimes advantageous to paint or spray walls white. This serves two purposes:

1. If several types of brick exist, or odd shapes, and uneven patches of discolouration—say, blackish in one part, reddish in another, a white or light wash or paint will have a unifying effect.

2. But probably the most important advantage concerns light. White paint reflects sunlight.

Hang baskets on brackets, and have them bright with colour all summer. Have boxes and pots against the walls, and fill them with bulbs for spring and bedding plants for summer. Create your own colourful picture—making sure that the prettiest pots are within view of an open door or window.

Light blocked by conifers or large trees. A line of tall *Chamaecyparis lawsoniana* can be an agreeable feature or otherwise, according to your point of view. They can provide seclusion and a private wooded atmosphere; but may also block out light and sunshine. The sacrifice is occasionally worth it, as shady patios and gardens can be very peaceful places, and a joy to sit out in on a hot summer's day.

Wind. Besides providing seclusion, screen walling, or trellis supporting plants, will give welcome shelter from winds.

In early spring or late summer, it is pleasant to sit out on a protected patio, when it would be considered uncomfortable in the middle of the lawn or elsewhere in the garden.

Bare walls or screen walling can be made to look more appealing with the addition of delicate annual or perennial climbers. Plant *Ipomoea*, the beautiful morning glory, and the purple or white cup-and-saucer vine. Or where there is provision for shade at the roots, the more permanent *Clematis* will not only grow well, but decorate the wall with wide-open, white, blue, pink or purple flowers in their season.

You may find, also, that the thin trumpet blooms of petunias will do better in baskets or boxes which are out of the wind.

Sun-baked stone. If your patio is an absolute sun-trap, your main problem could be to provide sufficient shade.

You can create this shade by using blinds and large umbrellas, and you are fortunate in that you can grow sun-loving subjects such as the succulent *Agave americana;* and have a collection of wide pans containing sedums and sempervivums. This sunny situation would also suit exotic fruits, for example: figs, pomegranates, kumquats, loquats.

Choice of plants for hiding ugly features. Unsightly walls, garages, or oil tanks can be successfully masked by the skilful use of climbing plants.

It is surprising what can be done. Sometimes the side of a garage forms part of a patio or terrace garden. This then makes a splendid background for climbing clematis, honeysuckles, ivies, nasturtiums, roses, or Russian vines. A look in the A–Z section will show which plants are suited to your particular aspect: south, east, north or west-facing. Better results are always obtained by putting a plant in the right place. They vary considerably in their individual requirements.

Where concrete or paving extends right up to walls, make full use of troughs, and square or oblong containers. Or build a raised bed along sides and in corners. Boxes may also be made with timber. These are sometimes used in place of raised beds; or at higher levels on a wall, as window boxes. Where raised beds are made ensure that your soil level is lower than the damp proof course, or this could be rendered ineffective, thus allowing damp to penetrate your walls.

Climbing plants may be arranged in containers so that eventually they cover the entire sides of unsightly buildings. Honeysuckle has been seen weaving its way through Virginia creeper—getting a grip, so as to reach quite a height.

Another possibility, not mentioned above, is the trumpet creeper, *Campsis radicans*. This climbing shrub makes a wonderful display right up the wall of a house, or out-house, if given a warm place to grow in full sun. Red, narrow flowers are produced in great number in late summer. There are pretty pinnate leaves too. Specimens can be raised from seed; and although it needs cover the first winter, it isn't a difficult plant to grow.

A pool on the patio

A garden pond or pool can provide an interesting focal point for the larger patio, and can have a beneficial cooling effect and assist in keeping the humidity at a reasonable level. Some pools can incorporate a fountain and the gentle tinkling of water has a refreshing sound in itself on a hot day; others support flowers of many kinds including magnificent water lilies. With fibreglass containers readily available it is very easy to provide a pool economically; but whichever type of structure you decide upon, there are some basic questions to consider.

Among the points worth considering is the question of water and how it is to be changed, or indeed whether it needs to be changed. With sufficient plant life in your pool, the water should keep fresh and be able to support fish.

An informal pool. The siting of the pool is important. If cleaning is not to be a constant chore it must be sited well away from trees whose falling leaves will contaminate it. On a small patio, the pool is best set to one side to provide interest but still allow free movement over most of the patio area. Alternatively, it can be positioned in the garden where it can be easily seen from the patio. Once the site has been decided upon the work can begin.

After removing any grass turf, which should be stacked to one side, the soil should be dug out to a depth of 30 in. (75 cm.) then lay a 2 in. (5 cm.) thick layer of concrete with a fairly smooth finish. On top of this, place a polythene sheet; and, on the polythene, cast a 4 in. (10 cm.) base. Large pools may need a wire mesh reinforcement in the base. Concrete pools built in this way are rather permanent constructions and cannot be moved, but they sometimes prove to be cheaper to build than their prefabricated counterparts.

The prefabricated pools are very much easier to instal and can easily be re-sited. Most are light in weight and are therefore easy to handle. Once installed they can be stocked with fish immediately with no waiting for concrete to 'cure', provided sufficient aeration is given by use of a fountain. Fish kept in pools need to be regularly fed until a natural supply of food is built up.

In the centre or to one side of the pool, you could have a small figure or other sculpture. Some can be purchased with a green copper appearance, as though they had been under water for centuries, and these blend in well with patio-pool surroundings. If you want something really special you may be able to buy the services of local talent, in which case, an art school is often a good place to begin your search for the unusual or the unique. Paving set to overhang the edges of the pool gives it a more natural look and there are many varieties of stone available.

Both around the pool and in the pool, white and cream water flowers could wave in the wind. And little red fish swim to and fro among the plants with the sun making its own pattern of light on the ripples of the water.

An impressive background to the pool can be made with a rock garden feature. But to look natural, great care needs to be taken when placing the rocks. Some rocks show strata marks and these should all 'flow' in the same direction as they would in nature. Rocks should be carefully arranged and the soil packed into the interstices between them. It helps if any protruding rocks have a slight backward slope as this enables rainwater to run back into the 'outcrop' itself and provide plants with an adequate water supply, and avoids soil erosion.

Exquisite alpine plants can be encouraged to send their roots into the cavities, but it is better to begin with a seed sown in a soil-filled crevice.

A formal pool. This is a job for a keen handyman, a professional builder, or garden construction expert.

First you dig out the hole—as for the informal pool, except that the sides will be straight, and the design probably square or rectangular. The soil is levelled and a 2 in. (5 cm.) layer of concrete placed as before. Then a wooden frame is constructed to hold the concrete lining in place while it dries. At the concrete-laying stage, you might like to allow for a shallow area towards the sides, which would be useful for marginal plants.

You will also need to consider whether or not you are going to include a pipe for a fountain pump and/or drainage pipes and locks.

Water plants. Remember to 'cure' new concrete pools before buying plants or fish. If loose lime washes into the water, it may kill them. The water should be left for six months before being removed and the pool re-filled. Or you can purchase chemicals which speed up the curing process.

When all is ready, choose your water-lilies and plant them in baskets, rather than in soil at the bottom of the pool. You will find this the simplest method. Use tiny pebbles to keep the cow-manure compost and soil in place. The cow-manure should be very old and mixed with loam.

Marginal water plants can be planted in ordinary loam compost in shallow baskets and these can be placed on a shelf at the water's edge. There are many excellent oxygenating plants that will help to keep your water fresh. Among the large variety available is:

Ranunculus aquatilis which has tiny, white flowers that appear on the surface; some leaves float, whilst some thread their way through the water on long stems.

Selection of hardy water lilies. It is not true that a depth of more than 24 in. (60 cm.) is essential for water lilies. If you select the right variety, you will find plants grow in 6 in. (15 cm.) of water in a little pool.

Nymphaea alba is only suitable for the larger pools —water depth 2–4 ft.

N. pygmaea alba is a miniature for 6 in. (15 cm.) of water. White, scented flowers are produced in profusion.

Hardy hybrids include:

Escarboucle: red with gold flowers; dark green foliage. Good for water depth of 18–24 in. (45–60 cm.).

Nymphaea laydekeri 'Fulgens' is another red with dark leaves. Water depth 1–1½ ft. (30–45 cm.).

Nymphaea marliacea 'Albida' is a white hybrid. Perfect for 12–24 in. (30–60 cm.) of water in the white and cream garden, as it never fails to flower.

N. pygmaea 'Helvola'. Tiny plant for 6–12 in. (15–30 cm.) of water. Small cream flowers. Recommended for patio pools. 'Gonnêre' has white, semi-double flowers. Blooms freely. 'Sunrise' is a popular, yellow-flowering variety for a water depth of 12–18 in. (30–45 cm.) of water. Fragrant. Useful for a shallow pool.

'William Falconer' has a deep, red flower. Same depth of water as above.

There are so many lovely hybrids. 'Rosea' and *Nymphaea marliacea* 'Chromatella' must also be considered for their simple beauty. 2–4 ft. (60–120 cm.) water depth required.

Always plant water lilies during a warm part of the year, putting the baskets of young plants on bricks so that they do not lie too deep.

Mature specimens generally flower from midsummer until well into the autumn. Very often the tiniest pools have the earliest flowers, as the sun warms up the water more quickly.

Selection of tender water lilies. There are some water lilies that seem as if they must come not only from another country but from another world.

In Africa, flowers of fantastic shape and size are to be seen in large groups—a shining, translucent sort of blue.

Nymphaea capensis, 'Cape Blue', has large fragrant flowers with blue anthers. Its natural habitat is Africa. 'Daubenyana' is a small, blue-flowering variety, which blooms throughout the summer. Suitable for shallow water.

N. burtii 'Blue Bird' has deep blue flowers raised above the water level, as indeed almost all the tropical water lily flowers are.

N. stellata has star-shaped flowers; and there are many popular hybrids of this species.

N. rubra. This deep red lily came originally from India; and has been one of the parents of the hybrid 'Devoniensis', a pinky-red with large flowers.

Selection of plants for pool surrounds. These 'marginals' or bog plants will grow well near the water's edge.

Irises are splendid plants to have near water. The sword leaves arise in architecturally pleasing smooth, clean lines. The sizes of species vary and should be chosen with due consideration to the size of the pool.

Iris setosa would be suitable for such a small pool setting. It is only 6 in. (15 cm.).

I. graminea is a medium-sized reddish or violet iris with the scent of ripe plums; flowers well in dappled shade.

I. japonica has flowers which rival orchids in their spectacular blooms. Not too tall at under 2 ft. (60 cm.); but needs a sheltered corner.

I. pseudacorus. The yellow flag iris is easy to grow at the side of a pool. There is a possibility that this iris may have been the inspiration for the French 'Fleur-de-Lis.' Try also 'Variegata' with green and cream leaves.

Iris sibirica flowers in summer with its flags opening violet-blue. Purple Mere is a lovely variety; or choose Snow Queen for the white and cream garden. The stems can reach 2–3 ft. (60–90 cm.).

I. kaempferi, like sibirica, requires plenty of moisture —even the shallow end of the pool if dry during winter. Also summer-flowering. 3 ft. (90 cm.).

No matter how large the pool, one or two magnificent plants—or groups of the same species—

will usually be more attractive than an over-crowded collection. Simplicity is worth considering carefully where water gardens are concerned.

At other levels, different plants may be included with beneficial effect:

Primula japonica is a pretty, deep pink flowering bog plant for a shady patch. Or the 9 in. (22.5 cm.) *P. rosea* might be planted just above water level, between the rocks at the back of the pool—to be admired at close range, or from the windows of the house.

Day lilies, or hybrids of the *Hemerocallis* genus grow well in part shade, part sun; but the leaves are rather untidy, so position this plant towards the sides. 24 in. (60 cm.) inflorescence stems appear in summer. Usually a vigorous plant.

Ornamental grasses. One of the best is *Glyceria aquatica variegata*, a green and white striped subject which grows about 12 in. (30 cm.) high. Keep this one in a sunny spot up on the bank. It will also thrive in a pot, where fresh shoots will re-emerge each spring.

Ferns. There is a dainty outdoor maidenhair fern, which I am quite fond of, called *Adiantum pedatum*. Its black, thread-like stems and tiny, bright green fronds, grow well in a damp, shady area. Try it between the water-side rocks.

It used to thrive for me under a hazel-nut, before the tree was moved. 'Nothing would it bear but . . .' inspiring catkins in early spring. So remember, when you are about to cut down the big, boring leaves in summer, the hazel *is* worth keeping for the catkins alone.

The strictly formal patio will have paving stones, or a similar hard surface—perhaps tiles or marble slabs—right to the rim of the pool. Three or four tubs, pots, or urns may be arranged to stand around the sides in a simple, well designed display.

Drainage

If you plan to build a large, formal pool, it is a good idea to lay a drainage pipe into the concrete base. The pipe should lead from the inside of the pool basin to a drainage pit filled with stones and rubble and about 3 ft. below the surface. The outlet of the pipe is protected with a wire mesh to prevent fish or soil from clogging it.

The drainage pit is constructed so as to take a quantity of water, and allow it to soak away quickly. It is usually filled with rubble, stones, loose cinders, or other non-coagulating material.

Does the water really need changing?

Small prefabricated pools are made without drainage holes in the base and the easiest way to keep the water in them clear, is to avoid using organic composts in a loose mud at the bottom, although cow manure which is well-matured may be included in submerged plant containers.

Keep a balanced collection of water-garden life, i.e., under-water oxygenating plants, fish, a water-lily, etc.

Leaves can be a problem in autumn, when the natural fall occurs. If you have a particularly pretty tree on one corner, you can use a net to cover the water when necessary. Water gardens should not be built directly under a group of trees since they need light sunny places in order to be completely successful.

Fountains

You will have to decide between a water-lily and a fountain, as these two features do not go well together.

Water-lilies thrive when the water remains at a temperature which is as near even as possible.

A water-garden in a tub

A gardening friend started with a large (60 gall.) tub—actually half a beer-barrel—sunk to the rim and surrounded by crazy paving. This housed a miniature water-lily and goldfish.

Fish

Goldfish. The ordinary *Carassius auratus* is a red-gold fish which does grow quite large if kept under ideal conditions.

It is the plain types of goldfish which prove to be the hardiest. They may be left out even when there is ice on the pool, although a hole *should be broken in the ice to allow gases to pass in and out*. A floating ball will often stop the ice from freezing.

Veiltails are fancy goldfish with shorter bodies and long, floating tails. These can be gold, red-gold, red and white.

Shubunkin is the name given to a variety of Japanese fish with pearly scales which reflect various colours as the light catches them.

The above are suitable for the small patio pool; but remember no more than six little fish to a pool roughly 6 ft. (180 cm.) in length; half that number for a 3 ft. (90 cm.) container.

Koi. In 1968, there was an important exhibition of these Japanese Carp in Tokyo. Since then, the popularity of the fish has increased rapidly, not only in Japan, but all over the world.

These 'Living Jewels' as they are often called,

are sometimes as long as 18 in. (45 cm.); therefore, although cold water fish, they do need a fairly large pool.

They are brightly coloured in yellow, black, red, white, and combinations of these colours. You will find that they make very good pets, coming up to the edge of the water to be hand fed.

Natural fish-food will consist of floating aquatic plants and daphnia, water fleas. But it may take a while for the water-garden to become established. Therefore put the aquatics into the pool before purchasing your fish.

Making a sink-garden

What is a sink-garden?

At its best, it is more than just a sink filled with soil and plants. The old sinks which were used in some cottages were carved out of solid rock; Cotswold stone (limestone) being commonly used. Clarence Elliot originated the 'sink-garden'. And it was these old sinks that he used—filling them with compost and rocks, and presenting them as miniature alpine gardens. They continue to be popular today.

Perhaps the most common mistake found in the sink-garden is seen in the selection of plants. Some kinds of alpines are particularly suitable for planting in troughs of any kind. But the types of plants chosen must be compatible with the type of soil used. There is no way you can mix *Cassiope*, or 'lime-hating' plants with 'lime-loving' plants such as silver saxifrages, successfully.

Also, be careful not to plant 'shade-loving' plants with 'sun-loving' ones, i.e. ferns with *Dianthus*. Choice, slow-growing alpine plants should be chosen—many of them little treasures, and quite rare.

Sink or concrete trough? You will be lucky if you can find a genuine stone sink, as these are scarce now, although some nurseries still stock them.

Alternatively, modern, glazed sinks, which may be obtained more cheaply, can be given a coating of peat and concrete mixture. This alters with normal weather action; and becomes almost natural-looking in a few weeks.

A concrete trough is yet another possibility. If you are constructing one of these yourself, remember to make drainage holes in the base. Mixing a little peat in with the cement and sand helps to create the old stone effect. Some plants may even root in the surface, in time.

Filling the sink. A carefully made sink-garden will last for years; therefore you will need to use the right compost and to provide efficient drainage. For drainage, place perforated zinc squares or broken flower-pots over the holes in the base, then add a layer of washed stones, or more broken crocks in smaller pieces, followed by a layer of peat. The sink should then be filled with John Innes Compost No. 2 (without the chalk for lime haters) to within one inch of the rim.

After planting, a final layer of fine stone chippings spread around the domes of foliage will greatly enhance the appearance of the finished garden. Some enthusiasts also add small stones—chosen for their rock-like surface. These should be put into place before the plants. Larger pieces of rock may be sunk deeply into the soil for best results. Rocks and surface stones help to conserve soil moisture during dry periods.

Alpine plants for sink-gardens. These are so numerous, that it is really a matter of personal likes and dislikes. A good alpine plant catalogue from a specialist nursery will be found helpful.

Single genus plantings are very effective. For example, you could have several contrasting species of *Androsace*. Some form cushions of foliage, which are so neat and compact that they seem as if they would be at home in a doll's house garden. The tiny flowers are dainty and in exact proportion to the minute leaves. The following are recommended for a special collection: perhaps for the smallest size sink, which can be put under glass to save the plants from the worst of the wet weather in the winter.

Androsace pyrenaica—white flowers.
A. 'William Dyke'—minute pink flowers.
A. 'Hirtella'—white.

Other attractive gardens can be formed with several contrasting species of silver saxifrage; or several contrasting species of *Sempervivum*. These plants are completely hardy. (See individual descriptions in the A–Z section.)

Mixed spring and summer-flowering plants for sink-gardens.

The usual way of planting a sink-garden is to select a mixture of choice alpines which are hardy enough to leave without cover during all seasons: dwarf conifers, miniature bulbs, cushions or domes of rosettes, and trailing plants. Skilfully done, this can be very attractive; but it is more difficult to gain a unified effect than with the single genus gardens.

Gardens in miniature are fun to build; and the gardener who puts together a good one, which looks colourful and interesting during all seasons, should be congratulated. He or she will probably be in demand advising and showing other gardeners how it is done.

More plants for sink-gardens.

Here is a selection of plants to place between rocks for a mixed display. They may be used instead of, or in addition to, the alpines mentioned above; but grouped according to their soil requirements.

Campanula. 'Mist Maiden'—tiny hairbell flowers.

Dianthus caesius. 'Of Gardens'—pink. Sun.

D. 'Little Jock'. Sun.

D. 'White Bouquet'—miniature white flowers. Sun.

Cassiope lycopodioides. White/brown flowers. Spring. Shade. Lime-free soil.

Dwarf conifers:-

Chamaecyparis pisifera plumosa nana—yellowy-green and rounded in shape. Slow-growing.

Juniperus communis 'Compressa'—a tiny, pointed conifer.

Picea glauca. 'Albertiana Conica' is a beautiful green-gold. An almost-perfect pyramid shape.

Frankenia thymaefolia. Thin green leaves. Little pink flowers in profusion.

Chrysanthemum alpinum. Carpet plant with white daisy-flowers.

Geranium subcaulescens. Little red flowers all summer. G.s. 'Russell Prichard' Slightly larger variety of above.

Lewisia. 'Birch Hybrid'—pink flowers on 6 in. (15 cm.) stems.

L. 'George Henley'—red flowers. Sun.

The sink with an alkaline soil

Cyclamen coum

C. neapolitanum

C. repandum

Dwarf dianthus (not necessarily in the same sink with cyclamen).

Iris reticulata

Sempervivum

Silver Saxifrages.

The sink with a peaty soil and no lime

Cassiopes.

Dwarf conifers.

Gentians.

Ericas.

Snowdrops.

Tiny primula species.

The sink in a sunny position

Crocus.

Dianthus.

Miniature roses.

Sedum.

Sempervivum.

Narcissus.

The sink in light shade

Cyclamen.

Conifers.

Miniature mossy saxifrages (these will grow in a limy or a peaty soil).

Chionodoxa (not too shady).

Snowdrops.

Miniature roses—middle to late summer flowers.

Primula allionii—large, pink, flowers; tiny stems. Spring. Some shade.

P. frondosa—little, lilac-pink flowers; mealy leaves. Some shade.

Sedums—succulent leaves.

Silene acaulis. Pink.

Spring bulbs for the sink-garden.

The miniature bulbs really need to be enjoyed in close-up. If the container is placed under cover on paving next to the house, it is possible to peep at the opening blooms on the coldest, or wettest days. And what precious, heart-lifting moments these are in the depth of winter, or early spring.

There are so many bulbs. The following are merely suggestions:

Narcissus minimus is the smallest daffodil; and therefore especially suitable. 3 in. (7.5 cm.) tall.

N. triandrus albus. Angel's Tears—another tiny beauty, not to be missed.

N. juncifolius—my personal favourite on account of its unusual scent. Miniature, small-cup narcissus—only a few inches high.

Chionodoxas. Bright blue, rarely white, flowers. A useful addition to the mixed sink-garden.

Crocus chrysanthus. 'E. A. Bowles' Flowers very early. Cheerful yellow.

C. biflorus weldenii—one of the small early species. Grey-blue stripe on white.

C. fleischeri has white petals which open wide to reveal a red stigma.

Iris reticulata. Large blooms on 6 in. (15 cm.) stems. Many colours.

Hardy cyclamen are very suitable for sink-gardens. It is easy to have species in flower during every season except, perhaps, one month in midsummer. Even then there should be some leaves on show.

I like to see areas of stone chippings between the carpeting plants and the rocks. Some alpines may be actually creeping on or over the rocks. There should not be too many rocks; and they should lie at a natural angle in the soil. One or two conifers—perhaps one pointed and one prostrate—add to the interest. And remember to select alpines for their flowering season, so that there is always a bud about to open, or a well-loved specimen already in flower. Bulbs can be arranged to come up and die down in the spring without any lifting or re-planting being necessary—although occasionally you might like to put in a new variety. Once the sink-garden is made up, it should be a year-round attraction, needing little attention.

Patio Furniture

Chairs and tables

Along with the patio revolution has come a new kind of furniture. So if you haven't been shopping for garden chairs for some time, you could be in for a surprise.

The cane chairs and deck chairs, valued for the way they slip quietly into the background with their soft lines, have become no less serviceable, but less popular. In their place have come great, gaudy chairs of lounge proportions carrying giant, puffed up cushions fashioned in dazzling designs. The idea seems to be that they should be as noticeable as possible. White zig-zag lines are sometimes splashed across vivid reds and oranges. What pale petal is going to compete with this?

But some of the patterns are attractive in the right setting. When the cushions are in plain colours, the modern hammocks look extremely comfortable with their fringed sun-shades, and their soda-tables at their sides. Or there are rocking-chairs with matching, bouncy cushions. These can be in a strong, blue canvas, studded at the back with buttons. They should fit into the modern patio scene. One can imagine spending a lazy afternoon with a good book beside a pool—gently rocking.

Breakfast, tea, or even dinner on the patio or terrace can be delightful. And many of the tables are tempting.

A display that caught my attention at a major exhibition consisted of an enormous table surrounded by enormous chairs, padded to perfection in deep red. The table was spread with red napkins and laid as if for an Alice in Wonderland tea-party.

Obviously, a very large patio or terrace would be necessary for such a long table and so many chairs. But where would all the furniture go when not in use, I wonder. Or would it stay laid out forever, gradually fading with the seasons? 'Curiouser and curiouser. . . .' The only thing missing is the glistening, green insect with black-dot eye, which crawls sleepily out of the cuckoo spit. We know it's not *really* cuckoo spit.

More suitable, perhaps, for the small spaces in many paved gardens, would be the strong, yet light, aluminium alloy tables and chairs, which are coated with a rust-proof paint. They come in thin, lacy designs.

Wooden seats. Another idea worth considering is to fix a wooden bench between the bricks of a raised bed on the patio. The wooden board goes across a D-shaped indentation in the raised flower-bed design. This can be very useful; and helps to make gardening enjoyable at any age. You could even sit down to do the weeding!

Otherwise, an ordinary garden seat might be fitted into a special corner, and pots or square containers placed on both sides.

A home-made table. It is quite an easy job for the handy-man to make a garden table out of strips of wood and any old chair or table legs that he happens to have available.

Ash-trays. One final touch to the fully-furnished patio is the ash-tray, carefully placed on the corner of a table, or on a solid foot-stool! There are some which have been cast in a cement material to give the appearance of sculptured stone. In one design, a nude nymph is curled round a miniature water-garden. Another shows a water maiden lying on a shell-shaped stone. One problem—you may not want to sprinkle ash on such lovely creations. They are made by a firm that specializes in stone art. (See Appendix)

Ornaments. There is a wide range of popular items: wishing-wells, garden benches, gnomes, statues, fountains, etc.

Personally, I am in favour of simplicity. You may, or may not agree with me, when I say that the less ornaments there are, the better: a few functional chairs, a table of some kind, some pots or urns, and possibly one sculptured figure—or on an extremely large terrace, more than one. But otherwise, I like to let the natural foliage and flowers provide the decoration; and I can look for hours at their intricate forms.

However, a garden has been seen with every conceivable kind of dwarf and duck on display—and it has a strange fascination for every passer-by! So there is always room for a novel approach. Individuality is what gives each patio its own character. The ornaments in your garden should be the ones that please *you*.

An unusual container for pink hyacinths and blue *Muscari*. The barrow has been painted to match the flowers.

Paving

Building a patio or terrace yourself can be a satisfying experiencc—and an economical way of obtaining an extension to your house.

The paved part of the garden can be used as an outdoor living room for many months of the year. In Switzerland, Scandinavia, Germany, and other European countries, paving is constructed close to the house in order that it may be used as a recreational area, and many homes have permanent tables and chairs outside.

To one side, squares or rectangles are left without paving so that they may be filled with decorative plants.

Types of paving materials. Laying paving stones is a straight-forward job if you follow a simple plan; but before you begin, it is best to take a good look at the various types of material available. Paving usually stays down for a long time! And you won't want to change your mind afterwards.

Genuine, old stone is highly thought of in the horticultural world. The stone used for paving is the sort that splits easily along its natural rock strata into even slabs. York stone is a type that does this; Westmoreland stone is a rock that does not split evenly in this way. (But it is used for rockeries).

Other types of materials which are often used for paving include: plain concrete slabs; coloured concrete slabs; bricks in patterns; tiles; cobblestones—alone or in combination with paving stones; crazy paving in broken stone. Hexagonal-shaped paving is also a possibility in man-made materials. And there are paving slabs with designs modelled into the surface; or there are surfaces which are rough in texture: ribbed, brushed, or exposed aggregate.

Do be careful when choosing mixed paving slabs in several colours. Imagine how plants will look against the various shades; and consider whether you will like the arrangement not only a year later, but for years to come. Remember the same pattern may exist for generations. It is best to select plain, natural colours if you are in any doubt. It has been found that rock colours are easy to live with over a long period: beige, stone, slate grey, buff, or perhaps a very soft sandy shade of pink in the right setting. Another important point: patterns in paving should be balanced, otherwise they may be unrestful to the mind—certainly to the mathematical mind!

A method of laying paving

1. Choose the type and size of paving slabs required—from 9 in. (22.5 cm.) square to 24 in. (60 cm.) square. (Genuine flags may be larger; they are very heavy, and difficult for one man to handle on his own).

2. Draw the size of the area to be paved on a sheet of paper, and mark the arrangement of paving slabs to the desired design, thus forming a picture of what the finished area would look like. Mark also the over-all dimensions, and the number of paving slabs required. Remember to order a few extra slabs to allow for any breakages.

3. When you are ready to begin the work, go into the garden and set out the area according to the dimensions on your paper. Then take 9 in. (22.5 cm.) long pegs, and drive them 3 in. (7.5 cm.) outside the area. Hammer one nail into each corner peg, and tie string lines.

4. Excavate between the lines, taking away 6 in. (15 cm.) of top soil, thus removing all grass and weed roots. Level the bottom of the excavation.

5. Place hardcore such as broken bricks, rubble etc., and compact well with a hand-rammer, which could be hired locally on a weekly basis. Compact the hardcore to the required level; filling the voids with sand and compacting.

It is best to allow a slight fall away from the house to provide adequate drainage. In any case, paving or concrete abutting the house walls must lie below the damp-proof course of the house, and below any air-bricks which may be present.

6. Starting from one corner, spread an inch thick layer of a dry sand and lime mixture (5:1) over the compacted hardcore to cover the area of two paving slabs. (Sand without lime may be used for bedding stone flags.)

Place the paving slab on to the sand and lime mixture, and bed it down by tapping with a wooden hammer to the required fall.

A spirit-level is needed to check the line and level of the paving stones as they are laid. A 24 in. (60 cm.) spirit-level is a handy size to use.

The gaps between slabs can be filled with a mortar made up of 4 parts builders' sand to 1 part cement by volume.

Weeds

Soil-indicator weeds

Natural soils usually carry a distinctive grass and weed flora. For example, on soils over-lying chalk, you will find the smaller fescue grasses, and crested dogstail; whereas, in areas where there is a natural lime deficiency of the soil as in some coal districts etc., the grasses called creeping bent and Yorkshire fog will be found.

Weeds tend to occur in one type of habitat—although there are those which will grow in almost any kind of soil.

But certain plants can give the gardener a good idea of the type of natural soil which exists in the district where he lives. For example, mayweed, corn marigold (now quite rare), common spurrey, heather, and, of course, the wild rhododendron, will indicate that the soil is acid in nature. Wild *Clematis* (old man's beard), white campion, buttercups, Jack-go-to-bed-at-noon (something like a small dandelion in flower) and wood violet will indicate that the soil is alkaline in nature. In addition, wild foxgloves will not be present on chalky soils.

Weeding. This should not be a problem on a patio. Raised beds, small borders, tubs, pots and containers of all kinds are easy to keep tidy—the odd weed shows up immediately and can quickly be removed.

Mulching patio beds with peat or compost is one way of keeping down annual weeds; and this method has increased in popularity in recent years.

Part Two

A-Z list of patio plants

A

Acer palmatum. A pretty little Japanese maple makes a useful addition to a terrace garden. There are several cultivars to collect; and each variety has its own leaf shape and colour.

Try **A. palmatum** 'Atropurpureum' for its plum-red foliage, or 'Dissectum Atropurpureum' for the more finely divided leaves. During the late season the leaves turn through such wonderful shades and tints. It is worth noting that although plants may be raised from home-sown seed, the seedlings do not usually come true to variety. Specimens sold in the nurseries and garden centres around towns are grafted stock, and this process takes time, so young trees are often expensive.

A single specimen may be grown in a tub, or in a square of soil left between patio paving slabs. Lime tolerant.

Achimenes. Sometimes called 'Magic Flowers' these delightful plants belong to the same family as the well-known African violets. They do need a certain amount of tender treatment, and will always be best behind glass in a cool climate.

However, they can be used as hanging basket plants outside in summer, if they are given a very sheltered position.

The rhizomes are rested dry during the winter. They may be kept in a frost-proof cupboard indoors. Take them out and begin to water again at the end of winter, placing pots on a light window sill. Be careful not to let the young shoots get too cold at night—remove pots to the inside of the curtain.

In summer, plants in bud and flower look delicate in small pans decorating patio tables, or they may be transferred to basket arrangements and allowed to trail from over-head.

Varieties to choose from include: the new Lavender Jade; Butterfly—pink; Moonstone—white; Peacock—pink with a purple and yellow eye; Cattleya—light blue with a white centre; and Vivid with magenta flowers.

The length of flowering time does depend on the amount of light the plant receives, although there should be no strong sunshine. Liquid feeding during the summer can improve the size and quality of the flowers.

Achimenes are worth growing to provide a patch of unusual summer colour, and they can so easily be over-wintered afterwards.

Agapanthus. African Lily. A giant container full of big blue flowers can be an impressive sight in summer. The stiff stems reach two feet in height and they carry large umbels of blooms. The secret of success outdoors is to choose *hardy* hybrids. Plants have come quite easily for me from seeds sown in the spring. But the seedlings do need some protection during their first winter. Recommended variety: Headbourne Hybrids.

Agave americana. An easy and spectacular succulent. The variety 'Marginata' is recommended for a pot on a paved area, since the long pointed leaves are boldly marked with yellow and green. A young specimen is star-shaped, filling perhaps a four-inch pot and suitable for a window sill. Later, leaves shoot upwards and become gigantic; and in a year or two a really large container becomes necessary. Protect from frost in winter. Propagate from seeds or off-sets.

Alpine Collections. Any area against the house or a wall can become the home for a hundred or more little plants in pots.

I have found alpine plants particularly attractive for this purpose. Here are some of the advantages: they are mostly small; they are often rare or unusual, which makes the display interesting; there are often a great number of species and varieties in one genus—intriguing to the enthusiast—something like variations on a theme in music! But to give a more practical example: silver saxifrages have so many different shapes and sizes of rosette; so many different ways the inflorescence stem arises; and so many patterns of flowers. A collection can give hours of happiness: peering into symmetrical leaf formations; pricking over compost; potting up seedlings; putting on the stone-chipping toppings. (See also under *Androsace*, conifers, *Crocus*, *Cyclamen*, *Daphne*, *Gentiana*, *Saxifraga*, *Sedum*, *Sempervivum*).

Androsace. There are over a hundred species of this plant, but I have found *A. sarmentosa chumbyi* particularly suitable for patio pots. It also does extremely well in a cold greenhouse. Pink umbels of flowers emerge on four-inch (10 cm.) stems from the centre of hairy rosettes in the spring. Five or six flowering rosettes surrounded by several 'baby' rosettes make a fine show in a small pan. Or a specimen may be planted out on a terrace rockery.

This species is hardy in cool climates, but it is better if kept on the dry side during cold weather. Remember not to water pots more than absolutely necessary in winter. A sheet of glass can be used as protection from cold, wet weather for plants grown in an open bed. But this is not essential if plants are in a sheltered position.

Anemone. To be drawn towards the exquisitely dainty flowers of the Grecian wind anemones, you really need to see them grouped in the semi-shade. *A. blanda* is an excellent plant for wide patio pans. The original blue is beautiful; but there are pink, white, and lilac varieties.

There are more than 150 species and hybrids of anemone, but another graceful one that I have in mind at the moment is the British *A. nemorosa*. I like to see these delightful flowers in drifts nodding gently in the slightest breeze; and in gardens the double, white form *A. alba plena* may be planted in little groups at the side of a terrace rockery, where it will look particularly pure and appealing.

A. coronaria comes from the Mediterranean regions, and is the florist's anemone we know so well. Colours include blue, scarlet, and white. St. Brigid varieties make flamboyant patio flowers for the sheltered spot in full sun.

The time to propagate the spring-flowering species is in the early autumn, either by dividing the tubers, or by sowing seeds. Thrives in warm deep loam.

Anthemis cupaniana is a year-round decorative plant suitable for raised patio beds. It is one of my favourites. White, daisy flowers appear on short stems above grey, ferny foliage. The daisies keep on coming all summer; and there is constant interest from the evergreen leaves. A good choice, also, for a position at the sides of patio steps, although it does need cutting back after the first flush of flowers for tidiness sake. Propagation is easy: take young, basal shoots at almost any time—but best in late spring. Pot up in a sandy/peaty compost.

Antirrhinum. Choose dwarf, bedding varieties and group them in tubs or troughs for long-lasting summer colour. Remove flowers as they fade.

You can grow your own plants from seed sown in early spring in a temperature of 60 deg. F. (16°C) Transplant into outdoor containers at the beginning of summer. Plants can be used to replace the early spring display of bulbs.

Aquilegia. Columbine. I have a dainty plant which grows semi-wild in a shady spot under a lilac. The flowers are lavender and green—lovely for flower arranging—and they come up year after year, requiring little attention. Indeed I could say no attention.

Dwarf species are useful for small pans; the bright blue *alpina* is particularly beautiful, as is *A. glandulosa jucunda*, an Oxford blue—rather difficult to obtain.

The showy hybrids can be effective in large pots early in the year. The assorted colours of their butterfly flowers make an eye-catching show through spring and early summer.

Sow seeds as soon as they are ripe or in the following spring. It will be more than a year before you see your first flowers, but after that they should bloom every year with no trouble.

Artemisia glacialis. The whispy, finely divided, silver leaves show well if white stone-chippings are placed over the sandy compost. The plant is easy to propagate, as almost every stem-cutting will take if poked into sand and peat in summer. Choose a sunny position.

Aspidistra. When grown in a giant terra cotta container, the variegated form makes a splendid summer decoration for the less sunny side of a patio. The long, green and white striped leaves seem all the better for a light shower. The airy conditions may cause your plant to produce strange flowers, when the time comes for it to be taken indoors again. Buds may appear in autumn or early winter. They emerge like eight-sided, green water lilies, and the flowers rest on the surface of the compost. Each petal is tipped with gold on the inside, and the interior is a rich purple.

Large specimens look rather grand on the patio, but they may be divided at root level in spring if desired. Otherwise, give liquid or tablet fertilizer through spring and summer.

Aubrieta. This must be the first rock plant that almost every gardener comes to recognise in childhood. It is often to be seen trailing over the sides of raised terrace borders—the little mauve flowers completely cover a spreading carpet of foliage. But do try other colours besides the common purple/mauve—all may be grown from seed quite simply. The variety 'Magician' is a deeper red shade. Sow seeds in early spring for flowering-size plants the following year. A good choice for limy soils.

B

Begonias are useful in patio beds, pots, troughs, hanging baskets and window boxes.

Choose the giant tuberous kinds for big blooms outside your door all summer. Start the tubers off in early spring indoors, and as the young shoots emerge pot up separately into individual containers. Place outside when there is no danger of frost. A partially shady place will be suitable, which is sometimes helpful as the bright colours give life to an otherwise dull area. But one word of warning: buds tend to drop if the compost in the pot is allowed to become too dry.

For beds at the edge of patios, sow seeds of *B. semperflorens* early in the spring indoors; transplant into fresh compost as soon as the seedling stage has passed. Plants will be ready to go outside in early summer. They are marvellous for mass display—tiny flowers cover compact mounds of foliage. In addition, the leaves can be bronze or green and this colour contrast may be used to provide different effects in group plantings.

Hanging basket begonias may be grown from seed or tubers; but make sure you select the pendulous varieties. Try Pink Sensation or Copper Flame Sensation.

Bellis. The garden lawn daisy is *B. perennis;* the cultivated varieties of these delightful little plants deserve a place in every garden, and especially the small garden. Colours of the button-sized flowers include all the shades of pink from red to white. They look pretty in small pots, or they can be arranged in raised patio beds, where they should increase by spreading—but not so quickly as to be a nuisance.

Dresden China (pink) and Rob Roy (red) do not produce seed and therefore plants are propagated by division. Seeds may be sown of varieties Pomponette (white to crimson) or Monstrosa (larger daisies) for flowers the following spring. Some years we have had plants in bloom for most of the winter in addition to the usual spring show.

Bergenia. Winter-flowering with large 'elephant ear' evergreen leaves and pink flowers. Its best advantage, perhaps, is that it will grow in deep shade. Suitable for a wide-rimmed, flattish pot. Several species and hybrids are available.

Bletilla striata is an orchid that can be flowered on a patio in early summer. Strong new shoots rise up from resting pseudo-bulbs in the spring. First leaves become large and pleated, then flower buds appear from the centre of the thickest shoots. There are six or more blooms per spike; each flower bud is purple, opening to mauvy-pink with a purple patterned lip.

Give plants a peaty compost and plenty of water in the summer. Pot-on every other spring as this orchid needs a supply of fresh nutrients to do well.

It is hardy in some areas; otherwise a cool, almost unheated room or greenhouse is the best place in winter. No water is necessary during the resting period.

Bonsai. The Japanese art of dwarfing trees. Seeds of conifers may be purchased and grown in tiny containers; by restricting the roots, the size of the tree is kept to only a few inches high.

In my own collection, I have a wild plum with roots that are twisted round and round into a strange dome, rather like a bee-hive. But there are other plants suitable for bonsai including: beech, forsythia, silver birch.

When pruning the young trees, always aim at removing badly formed branches, or those that spoil the balance of the design as a whole. Much of the stem cutting is done during the growing season, rather than when plants are resting; and it is best to do the trimming while the growth is thin rather than when it is old and thick.

Personally, I do not care for bending and wiring into position because many interesting results can be obtained without these extreme measures. My aim is always towards the semi-natural effect as seen when trees are found growing between bricks on a wall—only reaching a fraction of their normal height.

Hardy trees may be left outside as all the year round decoration.

Bonsai bowls. These are low ceramic containers, glazed or unglazed. They can be square, oblong or octagonal in shape; and colours are usually close to nature: green, autumn gold, grey, black, brown or stone beige. A full range of containers in different shapes and colours would make an unusual focal point on any patio. Many have intriguing little legs, which definitely add to the decorative appeal.

Broom does not at first seem suitable for patio gardening; but it is a convenient shrub to place at the side of a newly paved area to hide bare fences. Numerous whip branches grow from a bush shape to reach a height of over six feet (180 cm.). They are evergreen, which is another advantage, and the stems become covered with lupin-like blooms in spring—filling the flower gap between the wallflowers and the roses.

In our first garden, we raised a collection of hybrids from seed, and in three or four years our sitting-out area was secluded. In addition, we had so many colour combinations in the flowers: cream, yellow and red, plum-red and bronzy shades.

There are several species of broom. Those described here are hybrids of *Cytisus scoparius;* and it is possible to obtain named varieties if a particular colour is desired, for example: Johnson's Crimson, Lord Lambourne—yellow and maroon, Golden Sunlight— rich yellow.

Place young plants at least 3 feet (90 cm.) apart, as mature specimens do not 'take' well if they are moved.

Bricks. There are so many intriguing patterns which can be made with ordinary bricks. Lay them flat, on one side, or up-ended in place of paving stone. Or they may be used for making raised beds on a terrace to hold an alpine collection above ground level—this will involve gardeners with less backbending when checking over their specimens. But best of all I like brick paths—they remind me of the yellow brick road in the Walt Disney fantasy —seeming as if they could lead to the exciting, mysterious world of the imagination. This is especially effective if the path winds out of view, say round a weeping tree; but other arrangements can be equally evocative.

BULBS. All of us who have gardens know that new bulbs are apt to produce the finest flowers in the first two years after purchase. In the third year flowers are possibly more numerous, but not quite so fine; and thereafter, sometimes fewer, smaller flowers appear, until ultimately all that comes up is foliage. There is a reason. The roots are annual, and they search for food over a strictly limited area. The time must come when the soil will be depleted of essential elements.

The period of satisfactory flowering can be lengthened by feeding the bulb with an annual dressing of three substances: sulphate of potash, superphosphate of lime, and bone-flour (or bone-meal). These should be scattered over the growth area as soon as the leaves show above ground in early spring.

The two chemical substances act quickly and produce a marked improvement in the quality of both foliage and flowers of the current season; whereas the bone-meal is slow-acting, and operative over a period of years.

It is easy to forget that bulbs can be used in succession to provide months and months of colour around the outside walls of the house. Here is a list to show the natural sequence of some of the spring bulbs available:

Early snowdrops.
Tiny bulbous irises.
Species crocus—smaller and daintier than the hybrids.
Species narcissus—some very interesting flower shapes.
Snowdrops—late.
Chionodoxa—blue starry flowers.
Scilla—tiny bluebell-like blooms.
Tulips—species often flower before the hybrids.
Grape hyacinths.
Early daffodils.
Hyacinths—outdoor varieties.
Erythronium—dog-toothed violet.
Fritillaria—snakes-head lily.
Mid-season daffodils and narcissi.
Late daffodils and narcissi.
Late tulips.

Calendula. The English pot-marigold makes a jolly show against cottage garden walls. Or, a white container filled with the orange and yellow flowers can be effective in a modern setting.

Seeds are sown in the autumn to provide spring flowers; otherwise sow seeds directly into the containers where the plants will be wanted to bloom in summer. In this case, sow in mid-spring. Choice varieties include: Geisha Girl—a rich orange with medium-sized flowers; Art Shades—apricot, mango, pale orange, cream.

Camellia. Glossy, evergreen leaves of *C. japonica* are highly valued for flower arrangements. In addition, a specimen outside your window or beside a door will give year-round pleasure. The exquisite, glitter-wax flowers can be considered as an extra bonus, when they appear from the end of winter until early summer according to variety.

It is important to provide a lime-free soil, and the best way to do this on the patio, is to fill up a large container with a peaty compost. A position against a north-facing wall or fence is satisfactory —although I have found that mine do well in a west-facing situation. The main thing to keep in mind is that the early morning sun from the east should not touch the flower buds after a frosty night, otherwise they turn brown.

For varieties try: Jupiter—pink single, White Swan—pure white single, Adolphe Audusson—red semi-double. I think the singles look best as container plants; but this is probably just a personal preference. Donation is, perhaps, the most popular pink.

You can increase your supply by taking half-ripe shoots in late summer. Choose a peat/sand compost and a warm place for the cuttings while they are rooting.

Campanula isophylla, known also as Star of Bethlehem and Italian Bell Flower, is a favourite for summer patio pots and hanging baskets. What is not so well known is that this plant is hardy in most parts of the country. The blue flowers open wide on compact heart-shaped foliage. There is also a white-flowering variety 'alba' and a variety with green and white leaves.

Cut off the fading flower stems and rest during winter. Little water is needed for three or four months. In spring repot into John Innes Compost No. 2. A limy soil is tolerated, and stone chippings placed on top of the compost add to the decorative effect if the plant is grown in a half-pot or pan.

Propagate from two-inch (5 cm.) side-shoot cuttings taken in late spring, or from seed which is now available.

Canna hybrida. A useful medium-sized plant

for bright blobs of colour from mid-summer onwards. Rhizomes may be potted-up into large containers. Start them off early in a warm place indoors, or in a greenhouse at 60 deg. F. (16°C). They will be ready for putting outside in early summer. The best effects are gained by placing pots so that the flaming colours of the flowers show up against white walls. Choose the varieties with reddish coloured leaves.

Cassiope. An ericaceous plant similar in shape to heather—but different! The bell flowers appear in spring on wiry branches, which are covered with tiny scale-like leaves.

A north-facing position seems to be suitable. Pot up in small pans, and provide a peaty compost. Do not let the roots dry out in summer.

Chionodoxa lucilliae, Glory of the snow. Hardy spring bulbs; blue starry flowers are six inches (15 cm.) high. But there is also a less well-known eight inch (20 cm.) variety called *C. gigantea*.

Plant bulbs in the autumn in raised beds or terrace rockeries; best in large groups, and attractive when arranged between patches of cyclamen.

Chlorophytum comosum. The green and white striped spider-plant, so often seen as a houseplant, can be used as a temporary patio plant in summer. Aim at producing a large specimen with 'baby' plants hanging all the way round. You will find that regular applications of liquid fertilizer make a noticeable difference.

CHRISTMAS CACTUS (See *Zygocactus truncatus*)

Chrysanthemum haradjanii (See *Tanacetum densum*).

C. hosmariense has silver foliage which becomes covered with short white daisy flowers from spring until winter—most decorative in boxes, pots, and patio beds.

In foliage and flower, this plant is very like a slightly larger version of *Anthemis cupaniana.* One striking difference is that the tips of the white ray petals are straight in *C. hosmariense* but oval in *A. cupaniana.* Both these silver-grey foliage plants are recommended for permanent patio display. The leaves and flowers are attractive over a long period.

C. frutescens. The Paris daisy is a popular patio plant. Taller than the two other daisies just mentioned, it is suitable for a small tub. Shrubby specimens are seen every year outside Chelsea flower shops. Londoners buy them for their roof gardens and porches.

CITRUS Orange, grapefruit, or lemon trees in pots look exotic along a sunny wall in summer. Glossy leaves attract attention. Plants may be left out during the summer; but some protection against frost is necessary in winter. We have taken young plants through the coldest months on an unheated garage window-sill.

Re-pot in spring using John Innes No. 3—a heavy type of compost is really better than the no-soil kind in this case, I find. Return plants to a sunny position out of doors as soon as the danger of frost has passed.

It is surprising the number of enthusiasts who manage to flower citrus trees raised from pips, although of course this is always a gamble, as some seedlings will prove to be early flowering and others will not. But the flowers when they come are well worth waiting for, as they are highly scented and quite beautiful. The white petals have tiny yellow dots on the outer surface and the flowers are about an inch (2.5 cm.) across.

Plant ordinary pips collected from the family fruit bowl and germinate in an airing cupboard or on a sunny window sill in late spring.

Popular species: *C. limon,* lemon; *C. paradisi,* grapefruit; *C. sinensis,* orange; *C. mitis,* the house-plant calamondin with really tiny fruit—keep this one at 55 deg. F (13°C) in winter.

Clematis. A pink climbing rose and a purple clematis can transform a trellis in summer. There are many species and cultivars of clematis, but the deep purple Jackmanii is my personal favourite—probably due to early associations. I remember an outstanding specimen growing in a corner of a cottage garden. It stretched seven feet in one direction and four feet in the other. On one side it mingled with a pink rose, and it reached down the long garden from the other angle. Thick knots of stem twisted up against the fence and down again towards the ground.

Prune the Jackmanii group of clematis—and all summer-flowering varieties—during early spring. A light pruning is best for a big, old plant. But young plants do better if cut right back, then flowers will develop from strong new growth in late summer.

On my present house, there is a beautiful white *Clematis montana*, which flowers profusely towards the end of spring. The thick mat of entwined stems and foliage makes this a fine plant for screening. However, spring-flowering clematis are generally pruned directly after flowering.

By selecting clematis carefully, it is possible to have plants in flower from late spring until the onset of winter. Special selections most suitable for patios are Lady Balfour—blue flowers—late summer and autumn; Nelly Moser—pink with a carmine stripe—early summer; others from the Jackmanii group; the pink or white *montana; alpina;* and *macropetala.* The last three are spring-flowering species.

To propagate from your own plants, take semi-ripe young wood and cut above two leaf buds including a section of stem beneath the buds. Insert the cutting into a peat and sand compost in mid-summer. When finding a place for clematis remember the rule: roots in the shade, 'heads' in the sun, and you can't go wrong.

Climbing plants are one answer to the problem of seclusion in a patio garden. It is amazing what can be done with a few seeds, cuttings and container plants.

For a quick and easy-to-grow red rose choose the old Paul's Scarlet. It always gives good cover; and it can be raised from cuttings without the worry of root stocks and budding. Most side shoots will root in late summer.

If you prefer a pink rose, try Zephirine Drouhin, an old Bourbon, and for me almost the perfect climber. I am enchanted by the bronzy foliage which has no thorns; and by the semi-double carmine flowers which have such a strong fragrance.

My choice of a yellow climber, suitable for fence and trellis cover, is Golden Showers; flowers keep on coming from spring until late autumn.

And don't forget the honeysuckles, especially if you have a shady corner—the Japanese species will even flower on a north-facing wall. It is vigorous and may be grown from stem-cuttings taken in the second half of summer. Flowers appear from early summer until late October.

An unusual choice consists of a grape vine. Excellent results can be expected in the south or on a south-facing sheltered patio. (See also *Clematis*, *Cobaea scandens*, summer jasmine, nasturtium, morning glory.)

Cobaea scandens, better known by many gardeners as the cup-and-saucer vine. And no wonder, because the flowers really do look like a Victorian doll's tea-set. They can be purple or greeny-white—the latter being favoured by flower arrangers.

It helps to place each seed on edge sideways when you sow them in warmth in early spring—possibly at the same time as that other beautiful climber: morning glory. Choose a sunny position, and a big pot, and plant outside in Summer against a trellis or other support.

Coleus. The common name for the popular pot-plant species is Flame Nettle—although this plant does not belong to the nettle family.

Growing a selection of shapes from a mixed packet of coleus seed is one of the quickest ways to brighten up a patio or porch in summer.

The hybrids are exciting. Right from the four-leaf stage the red, green and gold patterns begin to appear on the leaves. It is fascinating to watch them develop.

An early sowing of seeds is best. Begin in early spring in warmth under glass or indoors. Without a specially heated propagator, seedlings can be raised on a south-facing window sill in mid-spring.

After germination comes the daily thrill of seeing how the seedlings are getting on. First you'll notice a pair of kidney-shaped seed-leaves. These are soon followed by the first pair of true leaves. It is fun spotting the colour combinations—especially in the Fantasia strain. In these there is not only colour variation, but intriguing outlines. Leaf margins are fringed, frilled and fingered.

Transplant seedlings into 3, 4, and 5 in. (7.5, 10, 12.5 cm.) containers as they grow, or turn them into large stone bowls in mid-summer for mixed arrangements. Regular feeding with liquid fertilizer is helpful.

If preferred, cuttings of individual colour varieties may be purchased from the specialists. Or select named cultivars, for example: Autumn, Buttermilk, Scarlet Ribbons. And remember, too, the golden brown shades, which sometimes look loveliest amongst the greens of the garden. Try Winter Sun.

You can also take cuttings in spring of any good hybrids which emerge from a mixed packet of seeds.

Collectors' plants. Fashions may come and go in gardening, but as long as there are gardens and patios—or even window boxes—there will be plant collectors.

It is possible to form a collection of any kind of plant, perhaps seeking all the plants in one group or family. But quite often an interest leads to further specialisation, and a desire to own as many species and varieties of one genus as are available, say *Cyclamen*, *Saxifraga*, *Sempervivum*, *Pelargonium* or *Fuchsia*.

Compost. Basically there are two kinds of compost, John Innes Mixture and a peaty no-soil mixture. That is, of course, if you don't take into consideration: sterile and un-sterile. All compost for container work should be sterilised.

Concrete. Do not despair if you find yourself with concrete instead of paving. You can hide much of the plain surface with pots and containers. Have living greenery on every wall and fence, and let the plants themselves form the interest.

Containers. There are many types of pots available for use in small gardens to-day: clay pots are to be found in numerous shapes from the tiny thumb pots to the giant sizes. They are not expensive, although one must be prepared to pay a little extra for fancy designs such as wavy or pie-crust tops or indented sides. Clay half-pots and pans are cheap—when you can find them—and they are so useful for alpines and low-growing succulents. A carefully chosen collection of both pots and plants will be found decorative on a raised part of the patio.

Cat among the tulips! Large pots raise the bulbs and link several levels of terrace in this attractive garden.

Then there are the larger containers: urns and bowls; sinks and boxes; tubs and troughs of wood and plastic. I have even seen old wooden wheelbarrows used as plant containers. Once you begin to think in terms of patio gardening—or terrace gardening—you will also start to keep an eye open for any attractive container which could be filled with compost and turned into a home for plants.

The more simple the colouring the better, as it isn't usually desirable to have a container which draws attention away from the flowers. Some of the old, classic, Florentine designs in natural terra cotta and stone colours make a gentle combination with camellias.

Long troughs are excellent for placing at the foot of garage walls or where there is no room for soil beds under windows. Climbing plants may be grown as well as low-growing groups of plants. Old chimneys are another possibility—often interesting with trailing plants hanging downwards.

CONIFERS (dwarf). In addition to alpines, little trees can be an all-year-round feature. The way they are arranged will make a difference to the display. Looking around suburban and town gardens, it is noticeable that conifers are far more popular than they were ten years or so ago. A really tidy approach to a new house has been seen, where two beds raised with a three-brick high wall, swoop round the sides of a paved area. The beds are filled with a peaty compost and dwarf conifers—several colours and shapes. In between there are groups of daffodils and not a weed anywhere.

Another way of gaining an interesting effect in the winter garden, is to arrange five or six rooted cuttings of different conifer species in one giant pot. Leave each individual cutting in its own small 3 in. (7.5 cm.) container and pack peat between the pots.

Many conifers can be propagated from cuttings taken in summer. Choose 2 in. (5 cm.) side shoots with a heel of older wood attached. Set the cuttings into a peat and sand mixture and place them in a cold frame—or a box covered with a sheet of glass. Warmth and shade are required. Rooting sometimes occurs within two or three weeks. New top growth—often lighter in colour or reddish—will indicate that rooting has taken place.

Here are four conifers which make a striking contrast in leaf pattern and colour: *Chamaecyparis pisifera plumosa nana*, *Cupressus glauco-viridis* 'Boulevard' *Juniperus communis* 'Compressa' *Picea glauca* 'Albertiana Conica'.

Convolvulus (dwarf). For years we had a white weed that used to race a blue morning glory up into the sky. It was the well-known climbing convolvulus. My husband used to say 'Someone will make a fortune by developing a controlled garden variety of that plant.' Well in a way the plant has arrived. Blue Flash is a low growing compact plant which has big bell flowers in a deep blue with a bright yellow and white centre. A grouped planting in a tub or other large container looks magnificent over a long period. And what could be easier? You only have to sow straight into your raised bed or pot in spring. Absolutely no coddling.

Crocus. Once you have tried the species as well as the large hybrids, you will become a collector. The species start blooming earlier than the hybrids, and it is possible to have a succession of pots coming into flower over many months.

Crocus tomasinianus begins to bloom in mid-winter, the mauve petals opening wide at every weak ray of sunshine to display the orange stigma inside. Try: Whitewell Purple.

Then there are all the dainty varieties of the early spring *C. chrysanthus*: E. A. Bowles—golden yellow with a brownish coloured base; Snow Bunting—white when it opens with a red stigma in the centre of a yellow blob of colour.

The Scottish *Crocus biflorus*, bears tiny white flowers with grey/purple petal stripes. They normally open in mid-spring. While *C. b. weldenii* is even smaller and perhaps more exquisite with blue-grey on the petals.

Varieties of *C. vernus*, the large Dutch crocus, can also be grown in containers. Joan of Arc—white; Little Dorrit—lilac; Queen of the Blues—lavender; Striped Beauty—white with mauve-purple stripes; and of course Dutch Yellow.

Plant the tiny corms ten to a small pan of John Innes No. 1 Potting Compost. If you have just begun to collect crocus, you can purchase corms in the late summer and autumn ready for potting up. I usually re-pot my corms every two years after the foliage has died down. Keep pots in a sunny place.

Cyclamen (Hardy species). One of the charms of collecting cyclamen is the idea of having plants in bloom nearly all the year. But their chief attraction may also be as autumn and winter flowering plants; providing colour from the end of summer to mid-spring. Many of the species will bloom freely on a north or north-east facing patio.

Yet another of the joys is that your collection will probably improve over the years. Individual plants grow larger every year—some become as large as saucers in time. In addition, new tubers will come from self-sown or hand-sown seeds. Tubers last for years and years; and even a small collection will give continuing interest for the whole of the owner's lifetime.

Begin with growing plants rather than dry, resting tubers; and purchase your foundation stock from a specialist nursery.

Cyclamen (Propagation). Later, you may like to increase your own stock by sowing your own seeds. This can be an exciting experience. It is not possible to divide the tubers and produce plants vegetatively; and so sowing seed is the only method of propagation.

After the flowers fade, capsules form at the end of the flower stems. In most species—*persicum* being an exception—the stem coils back down to compost level. The seeds must be protected from birds. They ripen sometime in summer, the capsules gradually darkening in colour.

I have had success with cyclamen seeds by sowing them round the parent tubers in pots. It is a good idea to sow at the end of summer. During the first winter and spring you should see some seedling leaves—there is usually only one leaf per seed at first—other seeds may germinate after an interval of months or years.

Cyclamen (cultivation). Give your plants a light, well drained, soil containing some well rotted humus. There seems to be some friendly difference of opinion among enthusiasts as to the best light conditions for pots and pans. My own experience indicates that excellent results can be obtained in a shady situation. The hardy species will do well on a terrace facing north-east.

SELECTION OF SUITABLE SPECIES. Choose *C. neapolitanum* or *C. cilicium* for autumn flowers. The four-inch (10 cm.) *neapolitanum*, also known as *hederifolium*, is at the present time the most popular of the hardy cyclamen. Plants are easily to be had in bloom from late summer until winter. The dainty flowers have thin, slightly twisted petals that bend backwards—a little less than an inch in length. Most of the flowers are in varying shades and tints of pink; but I do have a lovely pure white 'album'— the largest plant in my own collection.

Foliage in the *neapolitanum* species is patterned; and a different silver design seems to develop on every seedling. Indeed, this is one of the fascinations of raising your own seedlings. This and waiting for your first flowers.

C. cilicium flowers are a trifle smaller than *neapolitanum*, and the plants are a fraction less hardy, although they may be grown outside in the same place.

Choose *C. coum* for winter flowers. The leaves are more kidney-shaped than the longer, more pointed *neapolitanum* leaves. And the flowers of *coum* are more dumpy in appearance. They emerge from mid-winter to mid-spring—lovely to look at during a period in the year when there are usually only choice flowers to be seen, carefully cultivated by enthusiastic owners. *Coum* flowers are carmine or white. 'Album' often has a deep mauve-purple base to the petals.

Choose *C. repandum* for spring flowers. Scented flowers in red, pink or white usually open after *coum* in April. And *C. europaeum* is the strongly scented summer-flowering species. Carmine coloured blooms appear during the second half of summer. (Now correctly *C. purpurascens*)

Altogether, there are more than fifteen species and cultivars of cyclamen; but they are not all hardy. The above are the best for beginner's collection; or for the person who simply wants an all-year decorative display in patio pots and pans.

D

Daffodils. (See narcissus).

Dahlias are colourful plants to raise from seed at home for patio display. Sow seed in early spring indoors at 61 deg. F (16°C) and plant out in late spring. Dwarf Redskin is a recommended new variety. Flower colours include: lavender, crimson, yellow, scarlet, and orange. There should be some blooms by mid-summer from an early sowing. I also like the Double Pompon variety for round, ball blooms against a paved area close to the house.

Otherwise, buy dahlia tubers, and start them into growth early in the year. When the time comes to put them outside, remember to select a sunny position, as dahlias don't do well in the shade. Use fresh compost, and water regularly, removing flowers as soon as they fade.

Daphne is valued for its sweetly scented flowers and neat foliage. The smallest species are useful for clay pans, terrace rockeries, or raised patio beds. There are a great many to choose from: some evergreen; some deciduous—mostly hardy plants.

Plant them in the autumn in semi-shade or sun. Propagation is possible at home. Insert short, side-shoots into peat and sand; and place them in a cold frame during late summer.

D. mezereum is a popular species. It flowers very early in the spring, producing deep-purple blooms. These are followed by attractive scarlet berries. There is also a fine white variety which flowers exceptionally early.

D. odora is a late winter flowering species. At 3 ft. (90 cm.) it is quite dwarf against the medium-sized plant above. It needs a sheltered spot in full sun—better on a patio than in the open garden.

Datura. Angel's trumpet. A tropical shrub we have had for some years, came originally from a cutting which was given to us. It makes a splendid patio plant in summer, and an unusual house plant in winter. Long, sweeping leaves, which are soft to touch, give the shrub a palm-like appearance. Creamy, hanging flowers, 6 in. (15 cm.) in length are richly scented. They are sometimes produced in summer.

Cuttings taken from my plant root easily. Any side-shoot may be placed in a soil-less compost in spring, and roots will quickly form. My specimen is the species *Datura suaveolens*. However, the newly introduced *D. chlorantha* Golden Queen, should make a satisfactory pot plant, and this can be grown from seed. Eventually you will need a large container, as the plant reaches several feet in height in two or three years.

DECKCHAIRS may seem a little old-fashioned in these days of plastic reproductions of Victoriana and blow-up air beds, but wooden chairs with canvas seats still have some advantages; and they will last for years if put under cover every night.

It is surprising what a change of canvasses can do for the garden scene. Canvasses come in plain colours—red, blue or green—in addition to the often seen multi-stripes. Large stores stock a wider selection.

Try placing something in front of you to put your feet on—perhaps a stool to match the chairs. It's nice to be able to contemplate flowers in peace and comfort—even if it is only for a few minutes mid-morning and afternoon.

Dianthus should be valued as much for their green-grey leaves as for their clove-scented flowers. The genus includes the carnations and pinks, plus the dwarf and alpine dianthus.

A mixed collection of the species will give colour from flowers or foliage all through the year; although some of the rockery dianthus are not so good in winter but wonderful in summer. For example, Brilliancy becomes a carpet of red, dripping over stones and steps; but the foliage is plain green, and not strikingly attractive after the flowers finish.

The old, wild pink, *Dianthus caesius*, is better, as it makes neat mounds of grey, and looks lovely in winter. I believe this plant has been re-named *gratianopolitanus*, but will this long name ever be preferred, I wonder? Pink-fringed flowers are produced in profusion in summer. They are single and scented.

Going up one size in flowers, there is the fairly new *Dianthus* Magic Charms. I have had success with the variety which now comes in mixed packets of seed or in separate colour packs. There is a rich red among the colours that is out-standing; but all the plants form cushions of foliage, which cover themselves with large, single flowers by midsummer from an early spring sowing.

Old-fashioned border pinks are popular as an edging to raised beds. The double White-ladies is noted for its strong clove scent.

Modern pinks have been bred from an old-fashioned pink and a perpetual-flowering carnation. The cross 'allwoodii' became the first modern pink. Now there are many fine varieties to choose from, and it is best to obtain a catalogue from a specialist nursery, if you are interested in this subject.

I had a rewarding experience with a modern pink. I took the seed from just one flower and raised myself a fascinating assortment of new hybrids. Amongst the seedlings, six plants were very different from one another: specimen number one had grass-like foliage; number two had white flowers; number three had spikey leaves and white flowers with a red centre; number four was quite dwarf; number five proved to be a pink-flowering variety; and number six had almost blue leaves. The last plant thrilled me. A blue-foliage plant was what I wanted for winter pots and beds. The leaf is wide and the plant as a whole is compact. Doesn't this experiment show what fun can be had by growing your own plants from seed?

When you raise something you like, you may decide to obtain more specimens of the same plant by taking cuttings. Short stem cuttings of pinks root well if they are set into sandy soil in summer.

The same kind of fun can also be had from growing the alpine and dwarf hybrid pinks—so pretty in tiny patio pots. And you might like to include a group of carnations Chez Nous for their rich clove scent; or have hanging carnations in baskets, so that the fragrance drifts around at several levels.

White paint has been used to brighten this patio. Flowers include: begonias, pelargoniums, petunias, and a *Hydrangea* in the corner.

Digitalis purpurea is more commonly known as the English foxglove. There are many hybrids available, but perhaps rather strangely, I prefer the old hedge-row type—especially the white ones. White foxgloves are my choice for a semi-shady wall. They look lovely against the terra cotta colour of house bricks.

Seed may be sown directly into the soil along the side of the house in summer for flowers the following year. Or they may be raised in a nursery bed in the back of the garden and transplanted in autumn. Do not let the soil dry out in summer. The variety Foxy will flower the same year if sown early.

E

East-facing patio. In a large container, you could have a hardy climbing plant such as a honeysuckle with sweet-scented flowers, or a pink or white-flowering *Clematis montana*. Both plants could also be grown in a narrow bed next to the house, and supported on a wall trellis. And both plants can be kept tidy with a yearly prune after flowering.

A tub might be selected for a flowering azalea; but remember the roots shouldn't lie too deeply in the compost, which must be of a peaty nature as no lime is tolerated.

Large clay pots 10–12 in. (25—30 cm.) across can be filled with bulbs for a winter and spring show. Pink hyacinths with blue muscari make a pretty mixture. Or try my own favourite grouping of white hyacinths with hardy white violets.

Wallflowers planted in raised beds stand up to the east winds quite well. Plant your seeds in late spring so that the young plants can build up their strength and make strong, winter greenery followed by richly coloured and scented spring flowers. The young stock should be raised somewhere away from the patio if possible, and planted up into tubs and beds at the end of summer.

Fuchsias can follow on from the wallflowers as summer bedding plants. They are a good choice for a lightly shaded area, such as a basement patio or porch, or a bed in the shadow of a fence, or wall, for part of the day.

There are many new varieties to choose from—some for pots, some for tubs, some for hanging baskets. (See also under *Fuchsia*.)

Echeveria. There are over two hundred species and hybrids of this genus; but they do need some protection in winter, and are therefore only suitable for summer display on the patio. However, there is a giant variety, which is especially spectacular on a terrace or patio. It forms rosettes 8–9 in. (20–22.5 cm.) across when fully mature, and smaller rosettes build up into a fascinating pattern all round the parent, so that the whole plant can easily cover the top of a tub. Several flower stems emerge from between flattish bluey-green leaves. The flowers are pink-salmon in colour and they keep on coming until late autumn.

Propagation is easy as old stems send out baby rosettes from the leaf scars.

Little heat is needed to over-winter the plants and even giant pots can be carried inside a south-facing glass extension at the end of summer.

Elaeagnus pungens 'Maculata.' An evergreen shrub with yellow on the foliage. Useful when young; but will eventually grow to eight ft. (2 m., 40 cm.).

Erica carnea. A hardy heather for small pots in winter. May also be placed between paving slabs. Yellowy leaves; white or pink flowers. Unlike most of the ericas this species will grow in an alkaline soil—where there is chalk or lime present. Varieties include: Aurea—golden leaves, pink flowers; Carnea—pink flowers, early spring; Snow-Queen—white flowers, winter; Springwood—white flowers tipped with brown.

E. cinerea. This summer-flowering species requires a peaty compost and careful watering, as the lime in tap water may cause some problems. Rain water is best. There are some lovely varieties available: Golden Drop with bright yellow foliage; C. D. Eason with deep green foliage and rose-carmine bell-shaped blooms; and Velvet Night has dark purple flowers.

There are numerous other summer and winter-flowering species and hybrids, and it is worth considering foliage colour when building up a collection. Whereas it is possible to have heather in bloom during every month of the year, the contrasting foliage patterns and shades of green and gold play their part in providing the patio or terrace with winter interest.

Euonymus 'Microphylla'. A delightful little shrub. I have a specimen four in. (10 cm.) high in a pot. It is called 'Variegata' and has white edges to the half-inch (1.2 cm.) leaves. It looks decorative among dwarf shrubs and conifers; popular also for the winter window box.

F

Fatshedera lizei is an inter-generic hybrid between ivy and the so-called castor-oil plant *Fatsia japonica.* It is hardy outside in a sheltered position, and the variegated form has cream-white markings which make it valuable for decoration against walls and paving.

To propagate, take side shoots in summer and pot up in sand and peat. Place in a greenhouse or cold frame to root, and put pots into the open the following spring.

Fatsia japonica is an evergreen with big, fingered-leaves which make a bold design against white-washed bricks, and as it grows well in built-up areas it is often chosen for patio tubs.

You can grow yourself a specimen from seed. It is best to take young plants inside for their first winter. Cuttings taken from short side-shoots will root in a peaty compost if popped into a polythene bag and placed on a window sill.

Flowers sometimes appear on mature specimens towards the end of the year—white flowers in panicles 12 in. (30 cm.) or more long. They add to the interest and they even have a strange scent. The glossy leaves are attractive all the year round.

FERNS. Many fascinating forms are available. Try raising a selection for the shady side of a patio or terrace from a packet of mixed spores. They are a good choice for a north-facing fence or wall. Different frond shapes gain attention due to their variety both in colour and in size. Also in the way some young fronds uncurl from tight coils in the spring.

FERTILIZER. If you change the compost in your containers when you change your autumn and summer arrangements, there is little need to use liquid fertilizer during the following three months, unless you are growing greedy plants, for example *Datura* or giant sunflowers.

However, when plants are permanently planted, liquid fertilizer does help when applied according to the directions on the bottle. I make full use of several kinds of fertilizers. I find the tablet form often brings plants into flower, when they can otherwise be difficult, for example some succulents.

Remember tubs with perennial plants such as shrubs may remain for years, and apart from an annual top-dressing, the compost will probably not be renewed. Therefore, it is advisable to start with soil enriched with well-rotted manure, loam, peat and possibly bone-meal.

In future years, tap off some of the old compost from the top of the pot and fill up with fresh. This is called top-dressing and it is necessary where plants are too big to re-pot. Great care has to be taken so as not to damage any roots.

FIG. A hardy plant when on a sheltered wall. Specimens may be kept in 12 in. (30 cm.) pots. Figs grow into large trees if not so restricted. They make fine pot-plants, and yield rewarding crops of luscious fruit. It is possible for the figs to ripen on the branches in early autumn, but take care to provide sufficient water in summer, as pots do tend to dry out quickly when the sun is shining on them all day.

Varieties include the often seen Brown Turkey. Propagation is effected by layering or by inserting semi-ripe side-shoots in a peaty compost. The shoots should also have a heel of old wood attached. Use 3 in. (7.5 cm.) pots and place them in a cold frame or in a box covered with a sheet of glass. Transplant into large out-door pots eighteen months later.

Flax. (See *Linum.*)

FOUNTAINS. Sparkling water can be a focal point on a modern patio. Gadgets for formal pools set in between paving stones are readily available from most of the larger garden centres. However, it is worth considering two points before installing a fountain.

1. Falling water is very attractive to toddlers. I remember being drawn towards the splashing sound, and tripping into my grandmother's pond when I was quite tiny. Babies can drown in only a few inches of water, if someone isn't standing near-by to help.

2. Fountain water will blow in the slightest of breezes, and for this reason it isn't a good idea to have it too close to the sitting-out area. (See also General Section.)

FRAGRANCE. Lavender and roses are favourites for summer. But why not arrange to have fragrant flowers close to the house all year?

In winter, *Iris reticulata* gives a slight scent from large Cambridge blue blooms. And the white flowers open on Sweet Box (*Sarcococca*). They are small, but the scent is so strong that a cut branch will perfume a whole room indoors.

The early wallflowers begin to come out. They are heavily scented—so much so, that they attract honey-bees at the other end of the flowering season.

Spring sees the tiny *Narcissus juncifolius* into

Begonias provide colour during the summer. Here, a tub has been placed on a wall to display the large flowers.

flower. I never tire of this plant with its exquisite blooms and intriguing fragrance—quite unlike the usual narcissus scent.

In early summer, the first roses unfold their petals. Choose richly scented varieties like Fragrant Cloud, a hybrid tea, or Zephirine Drouhin, a climber. Mid-summer brings the clove-scent of pinks and carnations—excellent patio and terrace plants.

For late summer, have you thought of having the fragrant flowers of *Cyclamen europaeum* beneath a white-flowering summer jasmine? If there are scented flowers near the house, butterflies will fly to and from the buddleia blossom, which you may have further down the garden. Butterflies always come to buddleia.

All those hazy mornings and warm afternoons—the scent of flowers and foliage is everywhere; even lavender sends out a drifty perfume as you pass.

Into autumn, and the honeysuckle will still be in bloom, and you can have white-flowering tobacco underneath. Remember the white variety has the strongest scent. The reds and greens may be fine for flower arranging; but give me the old-fashioned scented type every time.

The last roses mingle with the scents of early autumn; and then you will notice the herbs with scented foliage.

Or perhaps the first precious bloom of *Iris unguicularis* will have appeared. And early winter need not be difficult, a fragrant flowering *Viburnum fragrans* shrub is tidy enough to plant at the side of patio paving.

You may have noticed that I haven't mentioned other old favourites such as lily-of-the-valley, hyacinths, violets, and there is no reason why you couldn't keep these treasures on your patio too, although there obviously has to be some selection, where there is limited space. It is merely a matter of giving priority to the plants you prefer. But do try to include a scented group for every season.

Plan to place a seat close to the most fragrant patch of flowers, so that you can really enjoy their presence in any odd moments you can spare from your work. This is why I still favour the old-fashioned deck-chair—it can so easily be moved around from patch to patch. Aromatic thyme is a good plant for spaces between paving stones. It will give up its scent as you move your chair around it. *Microphylla corsica* is even more aromatic; but has a great attraction for cats, who are delighted to roll in it!

Fuchsia. This is an important subject for the patio. I can visualize many small areas outside homes up and down the country, where most of the colour in hanging baskets, boxes, tubs, and pots comes mainly from various forms of *Fuchsia.* Indeed, I know many whole gardens are entirely devoted to the growing of fuchsias in the summer.

My own taste takes me towards the crisp sepals and petals of some of the new single varieties. For example, there is a clear outline and strong red and white colour combination in Satellite.

However, the varieties with double petals such as Morning Light and Lolita do have a charm that reminds me of Bourbon roses.

Some varieties are especially suitable for hanging baskets, for example: Cascade with white sepals and carmine petals; the red Marinka; or Swing-time with red sepals and fluffy white petals. Try also the tiny Ladies Thumb in window boxes, or troughs along walls.

Fuchsias for the patio are usually treated as half-hardy or tender plants, and only put outside from summer onwards. However, some enthusiasts do manage to keep their plants through the winter by covering them with compost bags or some other form of protective material.

In spring, water old plants and maintain a temperature of 50 deg. F (10° C) where this is possible. When the new growth appears, take off the young shoots and root the cuttings in 3 in. (7.5 cm.) pots. Later, you will need to transplant them into 6 in. (15 cm.) pots or directly into large containers of mixed plants for summer display.

Alternatively, you could grow yourself a collection from seed. These plants will not be named varieties of course, but hybrids from a packet of mixed seed.

You can have a lot of fun this way: there is always the chance that there will be an exciting new variety among the seedlings—a hybrid that has never been seen before. Sow seed early, keeping the tray of compost at a temperature of around 60 deg. F (16°C) and germination should occur within six weeks; seedlings should be potted on and ready to go outside by late spring.

If you should find a specimen that you like among your seedling plants, you may over-winter it in a frost-proof place and take cuttings from it the following year. It is a basic rule of gardening —and one of the rules which makes it so interesting—that by sowing seeds you can obtain variety and by taking cuttings you can continue to produce the exact replica of a particular plant.

Therefore in the case of fuchsias grown from seed, you can propagate from any single seedling which appeals to you by taking cuttings from it, and they will all be like the specimen from which you take the cuttings.

Fuchsia procumbens. This plant is not a variety but a little species, and a native of New Zealand. It is very small—only 2 in. (5 cm.) tall —with round to heart-shaped leaves and unusual flowers. The dark sepals fold back over a yellow-coloured tube, and there are no petals. But it is the large berries which are the main attraction among *Fuchsia* fans. You will find the plant hardy in most southern districts.

The spider-web houseleek, *Sempervivum arachnoideum,* is a hardy plant to choose for terrace steps or low walls.

Below

Yellow and purple petunias harmonize with the ancient appearance of the shallow bowl. Petunias flower all summer on the patio.

G

Gentiana. Some of the smaller gentians are suitable for pots and pans on the patio. They are perfectly hardy, although notoriously difficult to flower well in consecutive years. But because the flowers are such a brilliant blue when they do come, many people are drawn towards the best species and hybrids.

Gentiana macaulayi produces rare-looking blooms in autumn; each flower is a star-tube shape, appearing close to the top of low-growing foliage. It will grow in a shady position such as is found on a north-east facing patio. Peat in the soil is essential; and it seems to help if a small pot is placed into a larger one with the space between packed with more peat. This keeps the compost moist during summer.

G. acaulis is another popular blue type, flowering two or three months earlier. This one needs a little more sun and very good drainage with grit and small stones added. It will not flower in some gardens, although it is the familiar alpine gentian.

G. septemfida is a much safer bet than *acaulis*; but if you want a really brilliant blue, try G.m. 'Kingfisher' or one of its offspring—in lime-free soil.

G. verna is a deep blue, European, spring-flowering species.

All gentians must be shielded from the mid-day summer sun; and they are all easily increased by division of the roots in spring.

Geranium. I am referring, here, to the hardy outdoor plants, and not to the bedding or pot-plant kinds, which are known as geraniums, but should properly be called *Pelargonium.*

Hardy geraniums are not so much suited to pot work, as to planting in the strips between paving or at the edge of raised beds. I have three of the many species available.

Geranium ibericum has attractive blue flowers, but they are rather short-lived, and this plus the fact that the plant is untidy after flowering means that I cannot recommend it for the patio.

G. sanguineum, also known as bloody crane's bill, is better as the flowering period is continuous all summer. But not everyone likes magenta-coloured blooms, even though the plant is low-growing and otherwise suitable.

G. endressii is my favourite with pale pink flowers, one in. (2.5 cm.) wide. There used to be a bank of this in my childhood cottage home—perhaps it is the association that I remember with pleasure, although it also grows well in my present garden—originating from a cutting taken years ago in the cottage garden.

All these three species flower in the shade, which makes them valuable for positions sometimes considered difficult to fill. It is a good idea to cut back the foliage of *sanguineum* to encourage further flowers after the first flush is finished. It is easier to divide the plants at root level during winter—rather than take cuttings. In any case, cuttings should have a few roots attached. (See also Sink Gardens.)

Grape hyacinths See under Muscari.

H

Hanging baskets and hanging clay pots. First consider which type of basket you like best: some are made of wire; others are made of plastic with an attached tray for drips; others are made from white cane woven into fancy shapes; and yet others are not strictly baskets at all, but clay pots held in rope nets. These clay pots sometimes have a pointed base, making it impossible for them to stay upright without the net. This might be to add to their interest as unusual containers. Baskets of white wicker-work are made to hold an ordinary plastic flower pot inside. These baskets are very attractive although quite small, only measuring about seven in. (17.5 cm.) across.

There are various ways of making up a mixed arrangement in a large wire type of hanging basket. The old-fashioned way was to place a saucer at the bottom to help catch some of the water as it trickled through—baskets do dry out so quickly in strong sunshine. The sides were then lined with sphagnum moss and plants were poked through the wire into the compost in the centre.

Some gardeners line their baskets with polythene before putting in the compost, filling only the top with plants. But the best way is to place a layer of moss at the bottom, and then a layer of little trailers such as the ever-popular *Lobelia*—hanging out through the wire holes—then a layer of compost and moss, followed by another layer of trailers until the top is reached. The top is then packed with showy plants such as *Pelargonium, Fuchsia, Begonia, Petunia, etc.*

Hanging baskets are often seen under a porch, near a door, or fixed from a bracket on a wall. But when a basket is situated in an open, windy place, different plants should be chosen, from those selected for the basket in a more sheltered area.

The brightest displays in sunny places usually come from red or pink pelargoniums grown with blue lobelia, while fuchsias make a bold splash of colour in the shade; or dwarf busy Lizzie could be chosen to catch the afternoon sun.

Plants for a warm, sheltered spot in summer include some of the trailing houseplants: *Hoya bella*, the wax plant with creamy clusters of shiny petals best seen from below; green and white-striped *Tradescantia* that goes pink in the sun; yellow trumpets of *Thunbergia*—Black-eyed Susan, some people call it, on account of the dark centres; mauve-striped *Zebrina*, which will hang around until December out of doors; and even the grassy spider plant can be arranged so that 'baby' spiders hang over the sides.

Hardy plants to choose for all-year display are some of the intriguing varieties of the miniature ivies. And the white and blue varieties of *Campanula isophylla* are hardy; but they are only decorative during the summer, when the trailing stems become covered with one-in. (2.5 cm.) wide star-shaped flowers.

Hedera. Ivy. There are many fascinating foliage shapes and patterns in the new varieties. It would be possible to create a shady arbour with nothing else but ivy on trellis-work, and still have a very interesting place to sit. Not everyone realizes that even the ivies that are sold as house plants—perhaps in mixed bowl arrangements—are really quite hardy, and all of them can be left outside in winter. In fact, they do not do so well under hot glass, as they do in a slightly shady spot out in the open.

Some of the better varieties of *Hedera helix* include: Goldheart—green leaves with light yellow centres; Glacier—green/grey and cream leaves; Sagittaefolia—a favourite with arrow-shaped leaves; Green Ripple—like a child's drawing of Jack Frost fingers; and Buttercup—a golden ivy.

Hedera canariensis is another popular species. It is a Canary Island ivy. *Variegata* is a green and cream form with large leaves. This too is hardy outside in winter, although this is the one that many people think is tender. Only really severe winters cause leaf damage.

Ivies are propagated from short shoots taken in summer. Roots form in a few weeks if the cuttings are poked into a peat and sand mixture.

Pruning is normally carried out in the early spring, although straggly stems may be cut back for tidiness sake at any time.

There has been an increase in the number of ivy enthusiasts in recent years, and a new society has been formed.*

*See Appendix.

Helianthemum nummularium. In spite of the long name, this little rock rose is one of the easiest plants to have creeping over terrace stones. The tiny, elliptical leaves are evergreen, and the saucer-shaped flowers open from late spring until July.

You can have fun sowing your own seed, as the hybrids almost always grow to produce flower colours different from the parent. Bright tints of yellow, orange, scarlet, and red shades. If you happen to get a colour which takes your fancy, you can raise new plants that will be the same by removing unflowered shoots and rooting them.

Choose an open sunny position for mature plants; but cuttings will root in about a month if they are given some shade to prevent moisture from drying out round the tiny stems.

Helleborus niger. Christmas rose is the common name, but of course it isn't a rose at all. The flower is rather like a large wild rose in shape, growing on about an eight in. (20 cm.) stem straight up from the ground. Most gardeners treasure them. They are so welcome around the end of the year, when few big, bold flowers are to be seen in the open garden. And the leaves—as big as a man's hand—grow a foot or so above the ground throughout the winter.

Potter's Wheel is the recommended variety with bigger flowers than the type—about four in. (10 cm.) across. Plants are satisfied with half-shade, which is useful. I have found that a little well-rotted manure makes a lot of difference to the number of flowers per season. It also helps if you cover with a sheet of glass to avoid damage to the petals by drip and splash. The resulting ethereal beauty of the flowers is well worth the extra trouble. However, the glass is not essential and I have grown some lovely blooms without any cover.

H. orientalis. The Lenten rose is not to my mind so suitable for the sides of the patio or terrace as the Christmas rose. The plants are taller, and the flowers come at a time when the bulbs have begun to burst into bloom.

However, if you have a special feeling for

Lenten roses, there is no reason why a place near the house shouldn't be found for a group. Flower colours may be pink or purple; white, or white with purple dots.

The compost where *Helleborus* is growing should be moist during the summer. Both the species described above may be increased by root division. You will find that you are always giving pieces away to your friends, as these plants are very popular with flower arrangers.

Tomato Pixie and *Tropaeolum* (nasturtium) Whirlybird planted in pots. 'Whirlybird Mixed' seed also contains red and yellow flowering varieties.

Winter-flowering *Jasminum nudiflorum* photographed towards the light so that the normal yellow colour is slightly diluted.

Viola 'Jesse East' a prolific miniature, very easy from seed. Note variable arrangement of spots on the petals.

Nerium oleander and a pink *Fuchsia* in large pots balance the upward growth of the vine on the wall outside.

Herbs are valuable on the patio for their attractive foliage in addition to their widely recognized health-giving properties. They often have interesting leaf-shapes, although some are more suitable for places between paving than others.

Chives (*Allium schrenoprasum*) belongs to the onion family and has pretty, pink pompon flowers. The dainty leaves only a few inches high can be finely chopped and added to sandwiches or mashed potato.

Parsley (*Petroselinum crispum*) is another low-growing herb, useful for pots outside the kitchen door. Being so rich in vitamins A and C and most of the essential minerals, it is a good idea to encourage the family to eat some every day. Always have plenty of the curly leaves close at hand for sauces, salads, and sandwich garnish.

Other herbs may be chosen. I know there are garden-lovers who wouldn't go far from home without a sprig of rosemary from somewhere near the front door, because it is supposed to mean that you will always return. '. . . rosemary—that's for remembrance.' (Shakespeare). Mrs Jessop is the most popular variety; but *R. corsica* is even more strongly aromatic.

Yet others prefer all the scented species of mint near a door for people to pinch as they pass. They go away with fingers smelling of Eau de Cologne, apple, or lemon essence.

But my two favourites with highly aromatic foliage are rue and thyme. The leaves and the shapes of the plants are most suitable for patios. Both can be trimmed into shape if necessary—even with shears. (See also under separate headings: rosemary, mint, rue, thyme.)

Heuchera has been one of my re-discoveries. I've always known the plant since childhood, where it used to creep over crumbling rockeries. But I have recently seen that it does reasonably well in the shade of a north-facing fence. The low-growing leaves are evergreen, and they make good year-round ground cover. An extra delight being the fascinating patterns of the flower sprays.

The bright red variety Edgehill arranged with the white Snowflake will suit those who enjoy vivid colour combination. Whereas, groups of the salmon Splendour planted alternatively with groups of *Hosta* develop into a more subtle display: sprays of bell-flowers wave in the wind against the bold outlines of the big *Hosta* leaves. (See *Hosta* below.)

Hippeastrum. I have one of these giant flowers facing me at the moment. It is a gorgeous red variety.

The bulbs are often sold in boxes marked 'amaryllis' around the end of the year for flowering indoors during the winter. But not everyone realizes that there are different species of *Hippeastrum*, and some species will bloom in midsummer on the patio. In fact we have a hybrid white variety, which regularly flowers *twice* a year! Four flowers per stem in winter; two in summer, and each flower measures eight in. (20 cm.) across.

There are one or two rules which must be observed, and then success follows automatically.

1. When the flowers fade on winter-flowering species and hybrids, it is absolutely necessary to water the plant regularly, adding dilute liquid fertilizer every ten days. Only pick off the dead flower head, not the fleshy stalk, as the food will go back down into the bulb and help to build it up for the next season.

2. The green leaves should be placed so that they catch every ray of sunlight—either indoors on a ledge, or when the late frosts have finished, in a south-facing position outside. A sunny wall is best.

3. Feed and water all summer. If you have mixed bulbs in your group, some will flower during the summer months—especially if you have young stock which you raised yourself from seed. Hybrids often flower for the first time in the spring and summer.

We usually begin to dry off our winter-flowering hybrids at the end of summer—this is a month later than many gardeners advise, our bulbs seem to do better with the extra growing time. We then withhold water for three months: according to the date that watering is stopped. Sometimes the new flower bud emerges before watering is recommenced.

It is possible to build bulbs up to full-size specimens—bigger than a man's fist—by keeping them in the sun four months or longer in summer. And you can bring the same bulb back into flower year after year.

But raising your own hybrids from seed, that is where the real enjoyment lies. You can either purchase a mixed packet of papery seeds, or use your own by letting one of your plants go to seed, and waiting until the seeds are ripe before sowing.

Maintain a temperature of between 60 and 64

deg. F. (16-18°C) while the seeds are germinating—easy in the late spring on a window sill or in a greenhouse.

Keep the seedlings inside during the winter and outside during the summer, taking care not to let the compost dry out until the young bulbs come to their maiden flowering—probably three years after sowing.

If your seeds come from a hybrid bulb, you can expect the flower colours of your seedlings to be scarlet, crimson, white, pink and/or orange. It's so exciting waiting for those first buds.

There is something of the spirit of adventure, for me, in raising flowers from seed. The same feeling that is evoked by this line of poetry: 'We were the first that ever burst/into that silent sea.' You never quite know what the colours will be, or the texture, the shape, or the smell.

Hosta. There are many species and varieties of the plant some people call plantain lily. Flower arrangers love the foliage with its bold outlines. But the leaves also make natural, green patterns on the patio against paving. Plants look good when grown in wide-rimmed containers, or in beds along the shady side of a terrace. Mine are situated underneath shrubs close to a north-east fence. They never fail to delight me in the spring, when the crisp, yellow and green patches of the young leaves reappear fresh and new. They light up a dull area and provide ground cover at the same time. An extra benefit being the tall stems of lily flowers which emerge every summer.

Hosta fortunei has pale mauve flowers; leaves may be either yellow, edged deep green, as in 'Albopicta' or deep green, edged yellow, as in 'Aureomarginata'. Height is around two feet.

The leaves of *H. sieboldiana* are enormous, blue-green, and marked with indentations running length-ways, but it is not one of my favourites as it doesn't seem to bring light to the scene, as much as the variegated species; and the flowers are a washy white.

I prefer the wavy leaves of *H. undulata*, marked with white as boldly as if from a painter's palette, and the lilac flowers.

But *H. albomarginata* from Japan, is neat at 12–15 in. (30–37.5 cm.) and the perfect choice for the patio. The leaves are rather like the reverse of the last-mentioned plant, having light green centres with creamy-white margins; the flowers are lilac with violet stripes.

You can imagine the spectacular contrast a group of hostas will provide in the garden. Do try them, especially if you have a shady space that you find difficult to fill. They will grow in an alkaline, chalk or clay soil, and they need some well-rotted humus dug in around them every year.

Hyacinths can be grown in the smallest area outside the house. They are seen every spring in long rows along the tops of short double walls, or rather walls with a space left open at the centre for plants. Sometimes they are in assorted rainbow colours: six red; six orange; six white; six pink; six blue; six purple. Visitors enjoy the perfume every time they pass. There is a house near where I live, which has such a wall running for yards around the boundary of a paved area.

Another way with hyacinths is to group them in large containers near a door. Several of the same coloured variety look impressive when arranged together in a pot. My own choice is white. And here is my economical way with hyacinths, which can be expensive to buy.

The first year, I buy the best large bulbs for indoor display. When the beautiful blooms begin to fade, I take the old plants with their floppy leaves, and dig them in somewhere among the shrubs, where they won't be too obvious while the foliage dies back down. I give them some fertilizer in the spring, and they make thin flowers the following year.

During that second spring the bulbs build up their strength again; and that autumn the bulbs are lifted and used for patio display in their third spring.

If you have no space at the back of the garden, it is possible to have a large group of thin flowers in a pot during the second spring. I have done this myself as an experiment, and the effect is not too bad—in some ways it is rather charming; but you don't get the heavy heads of flowers. And do remember to feed the bulbs at all times while there are leaves present, either with fresh compost or with liquid fertilizer properly diluted. This way, hyacinths give pleasure for a number of years. But if you wish to purchase fresh supplies of bulbs for the patio every year, remember to order early so that you can have them planted out by early autumn.

Hydrangea. It is strange that everyone who has gorgeous blue varieties growing with no trouble in their gardens seems to hanker after the rich pink varieties, and *vice versa*. I, myself, have the pink, which are not at all difficult for me; but I do look rather longingly at the bright blue ones; though they tend to look artificial.

There is a reason why so many pink flowers are seen in one district, and so many blue ones in another. Pink-flowering varieties turn blue or half-purple when the roots are in an acid soil, whereas blue-flowering varieties turn pink or muddy-mauve in an alkaline soil.

The *hortensia* group of hydrangeas flower continuously all summer with big ball-like heads of blooms. And it is not always realized that they are attractive all year too, because although the leaves fall in autumn, the papery false or sterile florets remain throughout the winter, drying to a bronze-brown shade. And as soon as these old flower-heads are removed in spring, the young green shoots are already well-developed and decorative in their own way.

Feeding with well-rotted manure is always beneficial. It also helps to keep the soil moist. Hydrangeas need plenty of water. They grow in sun or shade; but I find they do best in half-shade with either morning or afternoon sun.

Hydrangeas are hardy in the milder parts of the country but in more exposed places it may be necessary to place them in a sheltered spot, or it may be better to give them some protection in winter.

One way to have blue blooms in a pink-flower district, is to keep your plant in a pot and dress the compost with plenty of peat and sequestrene. Similarly, pink-flowering varieties may be kept pink in an acid-soil district by growing them as pot-plants and putting small amounts of lime in the compost.

Propagation by cuttings is simple. These make roots in the summer and if left undisturbed during the following winter they will be young plants by the spring.

Interesting paved circles meander from the terrace.

This arrangement allows for easy drainage, and the natural colour of the outer container enhances the pink and silver plants.

Hypericum. (Rose of Sharon.) One species of this genus *H. calycinum* is a useful, low-growing, evergreen for ground cover in semi-shady to shady areas. It may be inter-planted with *Hosta* and *Heuchera* in difficult corners to make a year-round display.

However, the *Hypericum* is the fastest to spread, and will need cutting back every year or so if you are going to keep it in its allotted space. It is worth having for its fluffy flowers.

The mixed group will give you lettuce-green leaves from the *Hosta* in the early months; brightly coloured, spangly inflorescence from the *Heuchera* in mid-summer; yellow flowers from *Hypericum* in late summer; and *Heuchera* and *Hypericum* will be winter green. (See also under Patio: shady).

Hypericum may be increased by digging up and separating a few roots in winter.

I

Impatiens. Better known, perhaps, as busy Lizzie. But whereas almost everybody recognizes the popular houseplant, comparatively few people realize that the dwarf hybrids make splendid subjects for raized beds on the patio.

The old houseplant has jointed, slightly translucent stems bearing bright green leaves, and it flowers summer and winter on a warm window sill. However, numerous hybrids have been developed. The Imp varieties are good outside in the open from the end of spring until autumn. They are only 9 in. (22.5 cm.) tall, and colours can be white, scarlet, orange, rose, carmine, purple or striped.

Sow seeds indoors in early spring. Choose a warm place for germination; transplant to beds or pots. We have been successful with plants grown in a place where they received the late afternoon sun.

I. walleriana variegata is more decorative than the plain type. The leaves are a pale green marked with white. Orange and pink-flowering varieties are now available. Take cuttings every year to keep a supply of young plants with patterned leaves. Old plants become leggy over a number of years. Stem cuttings will root in moist compost or just plain water.

Ipomoea. If you have a south or west-facing wall, I do recommend you to try the climbing morning glory. 'Heavenly Blue' is as beautiful as sky—if it could be captured in cupfuls. New buds untwist into wide, blue trumpets held high to catch the morning sun. We usually have about fifteen flowers a day to watch—less on a cloudy one, more on a sunny one. To see them at breakfast time is an inspiration.

Seeds germinate very quickly. It is not uncommon to find the butterfly-shaped seed-leaves already spread on the surface of the compost the morning after sowing. For this reason, don't be tempted to sow too early. You should not put your plants out until there is no danger of frost.

Iris—*I. danfordiae*. Yellow, sweet-scented flowers are surprisingly large on dwarf plants. Winter flowering.

I. reticulata. Another bulbous dwarf—only 6 in. (15 cm.) high—which flowers very early like *danfordiae*. Both may be grown in small pans; but they are better in separate pans rather than in the same one. There are many hybrids including Cantab, a popular *reticulata* with pale blue flowers.

It is difficult to flower them from year to year, as bulbs tend to divide into lots of tiny specimens which are much too small to bloom the following season. But this does seem to occur more often when bulbs are in open beds than when they are in pans.

I. (*rhizomatous*). *I. pallida* is worth purchasing for the vivid colours of the variegated foliage. Green and cream sword leaves look attractive among other plants, or in isolated groups. Choose the variety: 'Aureo-variegata' and count the lavender flowers as a lucky extra in summer.

I. unguicularis. Formerly widely known as *Iris stylosa*, the Algerian iris is a valuable winter-flowering plant. Large, lilac flowers appear from late autumn to spring. I am trying it in pots, but it is better in a stony bed near the house, where the scented blooms will be appreciated. The 2 ft. (60 cm.) leaves can become untidy, but it does no harm to the plant if you trim them back to about half their height in the late autumn.

Ivy. (See Hedera).

Japanese quince (*Chaenomeles speciosa*) makes a compact bush in a sunny position, where it will bear attractive blossom in the early spring. There is a deep red variety, or white, or the more often seen orange. Rather ugly large fruit appears later in the year.

JAR. A tall Italian vessel will add character to a paved area. One of the most intriguing gardens I know consists entirely of green plants and overhanging trees; and in this shady setting with light flickering through the leaves, two large jars have yellow and green foliage trailing from their narrow tops. Other jars may be used in similar ways: stone jars, storage jars, pickling jars.

Jasmine. I have three of the species. They are all useful as patio or terrace plants in their seasons. *Jasminum nudiflorum* is the winter one. It becomes a blaze of yellow from autumn to spring and in addition the whip-like stems are evergreen, which is another advantage. It is a good choice for sun or shade, and has been seen growing right up to the eaves of a cottage, but plants may also be trained to trail over the side of a tub in a shower of stems and flowers.

In late summer, *J. officinale* is a really lovely climber to have near the house. Fragrant, white flowers hang in clusters against a background of finely lobed leaves.

The best way to increase these two species seems to be by means of stem-layering. It happens quite naturally if stems trail along the ground during winter. Roots will be found on a portion of stem, and this may be cut and potted up to form a new plant. I have been successful in raising plants from both species in this way. The summer-flowering *officinale* produces black, shiny berries; but so far I have not been able to grow plants from seed, although I know this is possible.

My third jasmine, *J. polyanthum* is hardy in sheltered warm gardens, where the attractive leaves make pinnate patterns all the year, and pinky-white flowers come in spring. But in cool climates it is mainly grown as a house plant. Then the flowers appear in late winter, when the plant is given a warm, light window sill. The buds begin to develop when the temperature reaches about 60 deg. F. (15°C) therefore the flowering period is much earlier indoors in a warm room than in a cold room; and much earlier when indoors rather than in the open (only possible on a very sheltered patio—in Northern Europe).

K

Kerria is a useful shrub for a north wall or fence. It flourishes in places where few bright flowering plants will grow—in shade, and on wet, heavy ground.

Charming, yellow pompon flowers cover the twigs in spring. My plants have been known to bloom for five months; but the normal flowering period is in spring.

The evergreen stems make an attractive screen—often reaching to 7 ft. (210 cm.) or more in height. But when pruning after flowering, take out only the old wood, leaving young stems to carry the flowers the following year.

Pleniflora is the popular pompon variety; but single varieties are also available.

L

Lavandula. Lavender is valued on the patio for its silver-grey foliage, its fragrant flowers, and its low-growing bush shape.

I have found that cuttings root easily. Any short, unflowered shoot will be suitable. The ten lavender plants in my garden all came from cuttings, which were just pushed straight into the ground. But patience is needed, as it was the following spring before new young leaves indicated that roots had formed, I put several cuttings in one place, so that the group was obvious, and not disturbed during the rooting months. One or two flowers developed on my young plants in the first summer.

When transplanting into the final site in the autumn, the first thing to remember is that a sunny spot is necessary—perhaps a patch beside terrace steps or against a wall.

L. nana atropurpurea is a variety with much deeper purple flowers than the old English type.

Lewisia. These medium-sized, evergreen, alpine plants, flower well when grown in an open gritty compost; or in one part peat, three parts stone-chippings or gravel, four parts John Innes without the chalk.

The plants are hardy if they are given good drainage. They require an acid soil and full sun. Collectors grow them in pots or vertically in dry walls. Flowers appear through spring into summer. The petals are surprisingly large for such dwarf plants. Colours include: pale pink; deep pink, rose red, white, brick red.

Birch Hybrids are popular.

Propagate by removing side rosettes and potting them up separately; or by sowing seed, which usually germinate in the spring.

Lewisia are fascinating plants; but in my view the winter rosettes of foliage are not so intriguing as those of *Sempervivum* or the silver saxifrages.

Lilies. Apart from the deservedly popular cottage-garden lily, *L. candidum*, there are many other kinds that are no more difficult to grow and equally rewarding. Indeed, in their season, lilies may well be the most spectacular and the sweetest smelling flowers in the garden—including the patio.

For the average lily (if there is such a thing) the golden rule is to plant on a site where its feet are in the shade—say of low-growing shrubs—and its head is in the sun.

The choice of varieties is very wide, and the temptation is great as one browses through the catalogue issued by a specialist firm; but one can't go wrong with the regal lily, *L. regale*—an easy, accommodating plant which may be left in the same position for many years without it showing any sign of deterioration. Your reward will be magnificent tall stems, bearing perhaps up to a dozen pure white trumpets, shading to rich gold in the throat, and with purple staining on the reverse of the petals. Yet *regale*, though one of the most beautiful lilies, is one of the cheapest to buy, in a few years you can have a score. If you allow just one flower to go to seed, of course carefully removing all the other faded flowers—you will have a hundred seeds which will germinate as easily as mustard-and-cress. If you give the seedlings reasonable care, they will flower in four or five years, and steadily improve with the passage of time.

A local friend has a collection of lilies raised in this way from seed provided by the R.H.S. seed distribution service. Among them one bearing the fine-sounding (but well-deserved) name *L. speciosum magnificum;* and the more lowly *L. martagon* to remind him of the splendid Alpine meadows seen during Swiss holidays.

As highlights in a patio setting lilies should, if possible, be given a place of honour; and by careful choice of varieties a long-flowering succession can be assured.

Lilies in pots. The pure, white flowers of the Madonna lily, *Lilium candidum*, look lovely in giant containers in cottage gardens, or in pots on paving in modern house surroundings. Plant the bulbs in autumn, choosing a sunny position.

Linum narbonense, an absolutely beautiful, blue-flowering flax. It is a 24 in. (60 cm.) perennial plant, which flowers in summer. Probably the best position is at the side or front of a terrace wall.

Stem cuttings may be taken for propagation in early summer; or the plant comes quite readily from seed sown in the early spring.

Lobelia. The little half-hardy species *L. erinus* is a favourite for planting with red or pink pelargoniums. Tiny flowers cover compact cushions of foliage. Plants are usually raised by sowing seeds early in warmth. Varieties include pale Blue Cascade, Hurst's Red Cascade, pink Rosamund, and my own choice, the dark blue Crystal Palace.

Lonicera. There is a honeysuckle for almost every situation; but the most useful in my garden is the evergreen, Japanese species. This is useful, as it will grow in the shade, climbing and covering plain fences with a pattern of green leaves.

Highly fragrant flowers appear all summer and autumn. Each bloom is not spectacular, but the scent is strong, and will drift into an open door if the plant is placed close to the house.

Lupins. I am not going to suggest that you grow the ordinary herbaceous lupin in pots, although a dwarf variety has recently been introduced, and there is no reason why this shouldn't be kept in tubs, if you happen to associate the peppery smell with pleasant memories as I do.

The plant that I am going to suggest as suitable for patios, or small island beds, is the seaside lupin. These light-yellow lupins can be seen on the coast not far from Aldeburgh. They spread all over the low-lying cliffs and down on the sand towards the sea.

The daisy flowers of this dwarf plant require bright sun. In the picture, a block has been used to raise the pot.

The flowers are scented, but the fragrance is not like the usual lupin smell. It is a sweet scent which attracts bees and butterflies.

It is easy to grow a specimen from seed, which may be purchased under the name *Lupinus arboreus*.

A barbecue made more decorative with climbing *Wisteria* behind perennial plants in the raised bed and *Hosta* in the corner.

M

Marigolds. There are three kinds: the English pot marigold (see under *Calendula*); the French marigold and the African marigold (see under *Tagetes*). The first type is hardy, and will survive the winter unprotected. Seeds may be sown outside in autumn for plants which will flower early the following summer. The other two types are half-hardy—seedlings shouldn't be put outside until after the last spring frost.

Mint. (*Mentha*). There are several other species—twenty-four to be precise—apart from the well-known *M. rotundifolia*, the apple mint that we eat in mint-sauce with lamb. Or sometimes the curly *M. spicata* is preferred for this purpose.

A friend kindly gave me a few roots of Eau de Cologne mint *M. piperita citrata* a few years ago. I find the fragrance of the leaves very refreshing. You may like to try drying the leaves and sewing them into squares of material in the old-fashioned lavender-bag way. Or they may be included in a pot-pourri mixture of dried scented leaves for placing in bowls to perfume a room.

The best method of growing mint is in containers, as the roots spread so quickly to other plants in an open bed. Or areas of a bed can be separated with up-ended tiles to allow several species of mint to be arranged in one patch.

Muscari. Grape hyacinths are actually closely related to the ordinary hyacinth. The flowers of the familiar bedding species are a bright blue. They remind me of beads clustered together at the top of a six-in. (15 cm.) stem. Flowers are easy to raise from bulbs planted in early autumn. Twelve bulbs fit into a five-in. (12.5 cm.) clay pan. Give them full sun and blooms appear in crowds every spring. Foliage is rather untidy after flowering.

There is an interesting yellow species, noteworthy for its scent, but hardly ever seen, called *Muscari macrocarpum*. Flowers emerge in spring.

Myosotis alpestris. Forget-me-not. Who doesn't prefer the common name of this plant?

My method is to sow seed—either newly purchased or saved from my own flowers—in late spring. It is worth buying new seed, however many plants you have in your garden. Forget-me-nots seem to come lighter in colour every year from home-raised seedlings. Fresh seed from a specialist nursery brings back the intense blue colour and large flowers.

Seedlings should be ready for transplanting into their flowering places in the late autumn. They develop into mature patio plants by the spring.

Arrange them between wallflowers or tulips. Remember groups of flowers can sometimes be more effective than lines.

The odd white or pink flower usually appears among the blue—at least in home-bred seed—but if you fancy a whole patch of pink, purchase a packet of Carmine King.

N

Narcissus. Under this heading come all the daffodils; all the small-cup narcissi; all the large-cup narcissi; and all the numerous dwarf species that look so pretty in five-in. (12.5 cm.) pans. To me it seems that it is the last mentioned which are so often forgotten.

Here, then, are some favourites—both from the large flowered and the tiny flowered varieties particularly suitable for patio pots.

My first horticultural prize was for large-cup *Narcissus;* but the only reason I won that time, was on account of the late date of the show—everyone else's narcissi and daffodils were dead! However, I won a prize again the next year with a pot of ten Sempre avanti; and in the third year I had a terra-cotta container filled with fourteen white flowers of Mount Hood. Both these varieties—the first a narcissus, the second a daffodil—do well in ten-in. (25 cm.) clay pots. They may be placed outside a door or a window on the smallest paved area.

Scented narcissi never fail to thrill me—flowers inspire thoughts of the rarest kind. Each year, I hold up a jonquil bloom, half expecting it to smell less sweet, to look less exquisite. Will it still have the same freshness?

The wild *N. jonquilla* or its varieties Golden Sceptre and Orange Queen, are strongly scented. *N. poeticus* (poet's narcissus) bears fragrant flowers towards the end of the season. The perianth is white and the cup rich red; the most popular variety being Actaea. Or for a highly scented *Narcissus* with double flowers, choose white or yellow Cheerfulness. This may be an old commoner; but it never fails to send up a grand show of blooms—several to a stem.

There are also many miniature species. My personal favourite for the small pan is *N. juncifolius*. The tiny flowers are perfectly shaped; and the scent is mysterious. If you are looking for a little daffodil, try the hoop petticoat *N. bulbocodium*, which flowers early.

In addition to the above suggestions, there are many new varieties: some with all-white perianth and cup; some with pale yellow centres; some orange; some red; and some with an egg-custard-coloured cup called pink—or perhaps I'm not being fair: it is more pink than this.

The all-green daffodil should catch-on with flower arrangers and pot-plant arrangers, just as soon as it becomes more readily available. But for the present, Green Island is a beauty; and in my view, definitely one to acquire. It is not new, but unusual with a wide, flat-cup face, and superior shape.

The best way to discover which *Narcissus* appeals to your own taste is to attend one of the large horticultural shows. Your local show should also have quite a selection.

Nasturtium, *Tropaeolum majus*, is a climber with yellow or orange flowers. The leaves are circular in shape, and peppery on the tongue.

Besides the climbers, consider the dwarf nasturtiums; the variety Hurst Red Roulette is recommended. A group of these plants in a tub will produce a splendid display. They may also be grown at the top of a low wall, as the compost is more suitable if it is on the poor side. A rich compost makes the plants leafy but there will be less flowers. The position chosen should be semi-sunny.

Plant seed in spring in pots, indoors in late winter, or directly into open ground in spring.

Nicotiana. The tobacco plant. An enchanting species for the patio is *N. affinis*. White flowers are strongly scented—so strongly that one plant will perfume a whole patio, especially on a warm evening.

The green-flowering variety is often seen in flower arrangements, and there are many other colours available; but I have not found one that can rival the original type for fragrance.

They make rather large plants—2–3 ft. (60–90 cm.) in height—therefore choose a side bed for a group by the house—although a single specimen may be kept in a seven-in. pot if necessary.

Plants are raised from seed sown at a temperature of 60 to 65 deg. F. Seedlings may go outside sometime in mid-spring, according to the part of the country in which you live. The species is perennial, but almost always grown as an annual. Occasionally, the odd plant will come through the winter to flower another year.

North-facing patio. For screening plants to place against walls or fences with this aspect, I would choose the winter, green-stemmed shrub *Kerria* for yellow flowers in spring. Jasmine would provide yellow flowers in winter; honeysuckle would provide yellow flowers in summer. And not only will these plants grow and bloom in the shade, but the yellow colour of the flowers helps to compensate for the lack of sunshine.

Beneath the shrubs and/or climber I would have either *Heuchera* for ground cover in winter, flowers in early summer: or foxgloves for giant spikes of pink or white blooms later in summer: or cyclamen to carpet the area with green leaves and crowds of flowers in autumn and winter.

O

Orchids. There are numerous hardy orchids, and indeed they are a specialisation in themselves. In this section I will content myself with recommending the bee orchids which have fascinating flowers that look like bumble bees. *Ophrys apifera* are pink and brown; and the plant does well on a limy soil. *Ophrys fusca* flowers appear in spring, and they resemble the honey bee. But there are many other hardy orchids which may be obtained from a specialist nursery.

Exotic orchids can be grown on a patio too. If you have always longed for some of the magnificent waxy flowers, but considered that a heated greenhouse was absolutely necessary, you may be interested in my experience with the miniature Cymbidium.

A plant was kept on a semi-sunny part of a paved area near the house with no cover of any kind from late spring until autumn. The yellowy-green leaves were not unattractive all summer; and there was great excitement when inflorescence shoots began to form at the base of the plant near the pseudo-bulbs.

The shoots developed rapidly once the plant was taken into the warm living room; and by Christmas six-inch (15 cm.) spikes were supporting eleven flower buds each. The plant stayed in bloom for two months.

New foliage shoots had formed before the plants were returned to their late spring and summer quarters on the outside paving. This was in April; but the time for putting plants into the open varies from district to district.

If you are tempted to try this experiment with exotic orchids, remember that regarding watering it is best to give the plants a good wetting, and then not water them for about a week. This is preferable to giving a trickle of water every day. Rain-water—whenever it came naturally—didn't seem to hurt my plants. In fact it did them good.

During the period the plants had to be indoors, I followed the same procedure regarding intervals between soakings, but I used cool tea in place of water. My room temperature for the whole of the period was 60 deg. F. (16°C) plus in the daytime and 50 deg. F. (10°C) at night.

If I appear to have changed from plant to plants, it is because there were actually three specimens: one flowering-size plant; and two young plants for growing on—all came through successfully, and the flowers couldn't have been more pleasing. (See also *Bletia*).

Right
Polyanthus plants give a welcome touch of spring colour to a trough placed against an old wall.

Bottom right.
This pink *Pelargonium* makes an almost perfect partner for the long vessel. Choose trailing plants for urns and jars.

Bottom left
Lilium Brandywine, an Asiatic hybrid, easy to grow in a pot or tub as well as in the open ground.

An enclosed patio with modern screen walling and coloured paving is shown with shallow plant containers and light furniture.

P

Pans. Small clay containers—less than half the height of ordinary flower-pots—are called 'pans'. There are also large sizes—width ways—which make useful miniature gardens, when filled with assorted silver saxifrages, or mixed species of *Sempervivum*.

Pansies are properly violas, but we will consider the giant *V.* × *wittrockiana* garden varieties here, and other violas separately.

One of the attractions in growing pansies is that they will stay in bloom all the year. Spring sown seeds should be flowering by early summer; and some will continue to flower all winter. But you may also sow seeds in summer for plants which will start flowering early the following year. Yet another method is to sow seed under glass in February—these seedlings will be ready to form buds before June.

Removing flower heads as soon as they fade helps to prolong the flowering period of each plant; and it is best to make a habit of doing this, unless you wish to produce your own seed.

Favourites include: Arkwright Ruby and Blue Heaven—popular red and blue summer-flowering varieties; and Celestial Queen—light blue, winter-flowering variety. There are also orange, white or single-colour varieties; or the mixed Swiss Giant strain.

Passiflora. The Passion flower is an unusual climber for the patio. A lovely specimen has been seen flowering all summer over a town front-door porch—quite unprotected by glass. The species chosen for outside use is *P. coerulea*.

However, always give these exotic plants the shelter of a south or west-facing wall whenever possible.

I have grown plants myself from speckly seeds sown under glass in late spring. But remember, that in cool climates seedlings need covering with plastic sheeting or straw in their first two winters. Or, it may be better to move pots back into a greenhouse, during the frosty months, while plants are young. If grown in a 12 in. (30 cm.) pot or tub, top-dress with fresh compost every spring.

Constance Elliott is a pure white variety.

Patio types. There are many different kinds of gardens. And I suppose we could say that every patio is unique. I hasten to add that my use of the word 'patio' includes any space that will allow plants in pots—from the smallest patch of concrete to the largest paved and pillared area used for sitting outside.

But I have noticed that apart from size, there are basically four types of patio; and these are usually linked to the garden beyond.

1. The tidy patio as part of the formal garden. Raised beds are often in set patterns; and a number of plants in one variety arranged in neat rows —salvias, marigolds, dahlias, etc.

2. The patio—more often than not called terrace—of the semi-wild garden. The informal look of the cottage-type garden is continued right across the paving close to the house. Rambling roses against brick walls intermingle with other climbers; and creeping plants trail over raised stones. Tubs can be filled with quaint, old-fashioned flowers like the white form of love-in-a-mist, Miss Jekyll, or scented white *Nicotiana.*

3. The artist's patio, where potted plants with brightly coloured blooms are placed against an enclosing wall.

4. The patio or terrace of the collector's garden; each plant is different from the next with hardly any duplication, and there is a label beside almost every specimen.

There are variations of these four types, of course, and a certain amount of over-lapping. For example, it is possible to have neat plants in terrace beds with a background beyond chosen simply for colour effect; or the reverse of this: bright colour on the patio against a display of shrubs, where every plant is carefully chosen for its position and shape.

Geraniums and petunias are still popular for vivid colour effect; and for little labelled plants see under the Collector's plant section.

The design of a patio will depend on individual taste and the space available; but ideally there should be room for a table and chairs and at least a few plants in pots. Remember that the paved area may be curved as well as square or oblong; and raising the level in places will sometimes add to the interest. Indeed for a sloping area an easy to maintain arrangement is to build more than one paved platform. Each platform may be in the shape of a baby's bib—the space in the centre filled with compost and flowers.

(See also under shady patios, north-facing patios, south-facing patios, etc.)

Pelargoniums. Trailing or hanging-basket geraniums, Regal or show geraniums, and miniature geraniums, park bedding geraniums, are all included in the genus *Pelargonium*.

Most of the geraniums we find so useful for patio pots and window boxes are called zonal pelargoniums. If you look closely, you will see a pale brown colour, which is the zonal marking.

Numerous varieties have been bred by experts. Zonal pelargoniums bred for their bright flowers include: Paul Crampel, an old scarlet that grows very tall—almost like a climber; Highfield's Comet—supposed to be Crampel's replacement; Winter White—a striking contrast; Regina—clear pink double; Electra—semi-double, crimson; and Monica Bennett—a dwarf with dark foliage and pink, open flowers. Hundreds of other varieties are available, and new ones appear every year.

Named plants are grown from cuttings to keep them true to variety; but zonal pelargoniums may also be grown from seed to flower the same year in salmon, pink, red, or white colours.

There is also the deep red Sprinter which flowers six months after sowing. And assorted coloured blooms may be expected from a packet of mixed miniature geranium seed.

Varieties bred for interesting foliage colours and markings include: Mrs Pollock—wavy cream with green and black; Mrs Quilter—kidney-shaped leaf with large brown area; Bronze Queen—yellow with brown zone; Mrs Henry Cox—pretty red, brown, yellow and green pattern; Happy Thought—large cream centre, creamy-bronze margin; Crocodile—green and white, rather like an ivy leaf; Distinction—neat, green with thin black zone; Friesdorf—also with black mark, but open, red flowers are produced freely. It should be noted that some of the variegated-leaf varieties do have attractive flowers.

Regal pelargoniums are very showy, having large blooms often patterned in two colours. Unlike the flowers of ordinary bedding zonals, Regal flowers appear mostly in the warmest summer months. Varieties include: Cezanne—purple-mauve blotches on white; Braque—pink; Degas—orange-pink; and Grand Slam— a deep pinky-red with a dark central marking—one of the best. What a pity it wasn't given the name of a painter!

Ivy-leaved *Pelargonium* varieties for hanging-baskets include: Crocodile—as described above with pink, double flowers; L'Elegante—a good one with mauve-edged leaves and crisp, white flowers; and Gay Baby—very dainty.

Pelargoniums are popular—perhaps *the* most popular choice—for large pots and tubs. Take stem cuttings of your favourites every autumn and place several to a small pot of compost. This way you can keep quite a number in a frost-proof room through the winter—without using too much space. When transplanted into bigger pots the following spring, rooted cuttings will make flowering plants by mid-summer. Or, small plants will develop from cuttings taken off older plants in spring. If you decide to raise plants from seed, you will find it best if you sow early; but seedlings must be kept warm, and in a light place.

PESTS. It is only necessary here, to point out the more common pests that you are likely to come across in every-day patio gardening. You won't get far without finding greenfly in summer. The best method of keeping your plants clean regarding these insects is to purchase a pressure-can of insecticide and use it at regular intervals. Thrips or whitefly can be a nuisance in a greenhouse, but they are not usually much trouble outside in the open.

Bulb fly may have troubled you. Only certain plants are involved; but narcissus and daffodil bulbs are susceptible. Previously, the answer was to burn all suspected plants on the patio; but recently, a new product came on to the market. It is in the form of blue granules, which you simply shake on to the compost. It also kills other tiny soil pests; but after a few weeks the substance breaks down into plant fertilizer, so there is no danger of chemical build-up. However, any chemicals which change the nature of the soil must be carefully controlled.

You'll probably see the odd colony of woodlice from time to time. Always remember to place a small square of gauze wire over the hole at the base of the pot; otherwise woodlice will creep inside the container and feed upon the roots of your plants.

Petunias. Garden hybrids come in so many colours these days: red, pink, mauve, purple, blue, navy, and striped or blotched white. Pure white petunias are attractive in a mixed group with other white flowers, say, geraniums and *Campanula isophylla*.

There are four groups of petunias: *Multiflora* varieties with a large number of medium-sized blooms on compact 6–12 in. (15–30 cm.) plants; *Grandiflora* with large blooms on compact plants; and *Nana Compacta* with smaller flowers on slightly smaller plants. *Pendula* varieties tend to have trailing stems and small-size blooms.

It is quite simple to raise a few plants for use in patio pots and baskets. Sow seed early in the season. Germination occurs at window sill temperatures and seedlings grow into young flowering plants in time to put them outside at the beginning of summer.

Three important points to watch: plants need sun and they are better out of the wind. They will continue to flower all summer if the dead heads are removed frequently.

Two large pots make a garden. Boat-shaped bracts of purple *Setcreasea* (below geranium) carry pink flowers continuously in summer.

Philadelphus, also known as mock orange or syringa, is so strongly scented in mid-summer, when every branch is covered with white flowers, that the whole patio seems bathed in perfume. The species *P. coronarius* is a favourite of mine with its creamy, single flowers. It may be grown in the semi-shade which is useful; and we have had success with the shrub in a tub at the edge of paving slabs. White petals gently floated down every time there was a slight breeze.

If you like double flowers you might prefer the variety Virginal.

Purple flowers of *Clematis* Jackmanii and the dark foliage of the vine contrast with silver foliage and trailing plants in pots below.

Pinks. (See Dianthus).

Pots—care of. If you prefer clay pots, it is a good idea to give freshly purchased stock a soaking before planting up with your precious plants; and always scrub them in soapy water, rinsing well, between one plant and another—if you use them more than once. This may seem like fussy detail; but it is surprising what a difference cleanliness makes both to the look of a collection of potted plants and to the control of pests and diseases.

Plastic pots are easy to maintain: they only need a wipe round when they are new; and after re-potting, the old pots are quickly scrubbed due to the shiny surface of the plastic. They also last a long time, as breakages do not occur often.

Large pots and tubs made of any material are heavy, and when filled with compost, plants, and water, can be difficult to move. In this respect, it is obviously sensible to decide where the final display is going to be required, before filling the containers.

Pottery. It is still possible to have hand-made containers to your own individual design. See list of addresses.

Primulas are a boon to people with shady or semi-shady gardens or terraces. The hardy species may be divided into alpine primulas, and the taller kinds suitable for the side borders of a patio.

Some of the alpine species are so dainty, that although they are hardy, they are better kept under glass. They do not have to be in a green-house; a sheet of glass supported by a simple wooden frame is usually sufficient protection from heavy rain and other weather damage during the winter.

The pretty *Primula marginata* is the one I recommend; and in particular the variety Linda Pope. If anything is too beautiful for words, this plant is. It literally takes my breath away every time I look at it. Lavender-blue flowers appear in spring. They rise above grey-green foliage, which has a scent like incense, and is in itself spectacular—every leaf having a zig-zag edge margined with silver.

Propagation of this variety is interesting, as it is rather unusual. Side-shoot buds—fat and short—are removed and used as cuttings. The cuttings are taken during summer, and rooted in a cold frame.

Just to illustrate the fact that Linda Pope is not only completely hardy, but it can still be nearly perfect when grown without protection, I will tell you that I once won a prize with a specimen which had been kept in the open for a year without a glass cover of any description.

Turning now to more commonly known species, *P. vulgaris* is the botanical name for the little yellow primrose that we readily recognise as a native of our cool climate and often see growing in woods. But have it in a corner of a terrace rockery, tucked away in a semi-shade spot, and you will feel your spirits rise every time you pass the flowers in the spring. I come more and more to appreciate this plant for its freshness and natural beauty.

There are named coloured varieties of primrose, for example Mother's Day in reds, blues, oranges, creams. I have found that these grow from self-sown seed around the shady patches of my garden; but they may also be transplanted into pots and window boxes for patio display.

Keep a place, too, for the popular Pacific strain of polyanthus. They are exciting plants to raise from seed, as there are many different shades available; and from a mixed sowing you never know until the buds begin to open, what the colour will be. Sow during early summer, remembering to keep seedlings shaded from strong sunshine. Set young plants in their flowering positions in autumn for display the following spring.

There are many other species and varieties of *Primula* besides these few suggestions: *P. juliae* is a bold, red-mauve flowering alpine suitable for open garden culture; *P. denticulata*, sometimes called the drumstick primrose, is recommended as another choice for the moist side border—mostly in rosy-pink shades. And *P. vialii* is unusual with a thick spike of scarlet buds on an inflorescence which is arranged at the top of a long stem. The scarlet buds open into bluish-lavender flowers, and considering the striking colour combination, one wonders why it is not seen more often. It can be grown from seed quite easily; and makes an ideal choice for a cool place.

This covers my own favourites, but if you are fascinated by primulas and would like to try a large selection, a catalogue from a specialist nursery would be found helpful.

Pulmonaria has all sorts of evocative names, many with a religious significance—Virgin Mary's milk-drops, for example. Lungwort is also widely used.

It is a hardy, low-growing plant with white spots on the leaves of some species. *P. officinalis* is useful for ground-cover under shrubs at the side of a paved area. Pink and blue flowers are present simultaneously on the same plant during spring, and the foliage is decorative for most of the year. This is another plant for the shady patio; but it will also grow in the sun. Most soils are tolerated. Try using a group in place of forget-me-nots for a change.

R

RAISED BEDS are taking the place of terrace rockeries in some gardens. A low wall surrounding a bed of compost makes the work of weeding and generally caring for precious plants surprisingly simple. The beds may be filled with bright, half-hardy plants in groups according to colour; or they may be used as a safe area for a collection of expensive or rare specimens. Or yet another way of gardening in raised beds is to treat them as rockeries without rocks. Some of the better known rock plants can be raised from seed quite economically. The following will form an interesting year-round display: *Aubrieta*, *Helianthemum*, *Dianthus*, *Saxifraga*, *Sedum*, *Sempervivum* and *Violas*.

It is a good idea to design and build raised beds on the patio where ever possible. Gardening is an occupation that can be enjoyed at any age—especially if the need for heavy digging is removed from the job.

Ranunculus ficaria. It is easy to mistake this golden beauty for a weed. Indeed the lesser celandine *is* a weed, and there is an unwanted patch of it on my lawn. But the cultivated variety Major has larger flowers and doesn't spread so fast. The bronzy-yellow cups completely cover little dark leaves in the spring. This is a fine plant for a wide clay pan, or a sunny place between paving stones.

Rhipsalidopsis gaertneri. The Easter cactus. This plant may be kept on a patio for most of the year. The flat, green stem-segments are not unattractive, although of course, it is the wheel-shaped, scarlet flowers that make this plant so worth growing. It is taken indoors for the winter, and buds form for spring blooms. The point of including it in this patio book, is that flowers will form every year without fail if the plant is put out on a patio from late spring until late autumn.

R. rosea is a smaller species, about 6 in. (15 cm.) in height, and it has pink flowers, which come a little later.

Both species are epiphytic in their natural habitat, and they do best in a peaty compost, which should be kept just moist. Propagation is simple—almost every stem-segment will root in a few weeks.

Rhododendron. The smallest kinds are suitable for a place on the patio. *R. forrestii repens* is my personal choice for a pot or semi-shady position in a side bed. It is evergreen, less than 12 in. (30 cm.) in height, and bell-shape blooms appear in spring in a rich, crimson colour. The taller Elizabeth is one of its hybrids, and a very lovely plant it is too. The bright red bells are borne in clusters in profusion.

But there are many other low-growing species and hybrids to choose from, including the evergreen and deciduous azaleas, which also belong to the *Rhododendron* genus. The beginner should note that none of the plants will do well in a limy soil or compost. In fact most will gradually die when the roots are surrounded by an alkaline medium. It follows that in a chalky or otherwise alkaline area. probably the only way you will be able to succeed with rhododendrons is to grow them in containers, or raised beds. This way you can provide a peaty compost and top-dress with fresh peat every other year. However, it is worth remembering that tap water may have the same effect as an alkaline soil over a period of time, and in such cases rain-water will have to be used. Sometimes watering with a sequestrine solution is beneficial, or use Maxicrop with iron which has the same effect.

To increase your supply of low-growing species and hybrids, young shoots may be taken in summer and used as cuttings. They are quite easily rooted in a glass frame or cold greenhouse. Set them in a mixture of sand and peat—twice as much sand as peat in this case. Plants may also be raised from seeds sown under a shaded, wood-and-glass frame in spring; but patience is needed as it will be a few years before any flowers are seen. Layering is the quickest method.

Rosemary, *Rarinus officinalis*, is an aromatic shrub. It seems to have caught the fancy of every generation. Great poets have written about it—including Shakespeare—and there are numerous folk stories about the plant's powers. A sprig of rosemary was supposed to protect against evil, and many believe that a stem picked from a shrub beside a door will keep the carrier safe until he returns home.

There may be something in herbal myths, who knows? There are certainly natural oils in every part of the plant, and preparations from the oil in the seeds are used in shampoos. Or you can make your own hair rinses by boiling a bunch of leaves in water. Allow the liquid to cool before pouring it over your hair. The leaves—dried or fresh—are also used in some meat dishes.

Choose the variety Jessop's Upright for a sunny corner near a door.

The dark vine contrasts with *Nicotiana affinis*, fuchsias, pelargoniums, *Lobelia* trailing from square container, *Sempervivum* with daisy flowers, blue *Echeveria*.

Roses. There are four or five ways of growing them on a patio. Climbing varieties may be placed against house walls or side fences; floribundas are suitable for dividing hedges; tea roses may be planted in beds surrounded by paving, or in tubs or pots beside steps.

For climbers, my personal choice consists of the champagne coloured Schoolgirl; the yellow, Golden Showers; and the fragrant, pink Zephirine Drouhin: all are lovely close to the house—but particularly the last mentioned.

For a tall, floribunda rose hedge, choose Queen Elizabeth. It is amazing how much character this plant has—the petals are a distinctive, clear pink. The stems are strong-growing and quickly reach a height of 6 ft. (180 cm.) or more. And the foliage really does seem to be disease-resistant.

Favourite hybrid tea roses may be kept in a tub or in a small bed between paving stones. And any of the miniatures are pretty in pots; but I will put in an extra word for Pompon de Paris, the miniature climbing rose.

When roses are grown in pots, tubs or containers of any kind, care should be taken during summer to provide enough water.

Other tips for patio cultivation of roses include normal feeding and pruning at the correct times. To prune, cut out dead stems, thin stems, and any that crowd the centre. Healthy stems growing firmly outwards may be shortened to about half their length in early spring—often in February or March, but depending on weather conditions and location. Well-rotted manure is probably the best fertilizer, but packet chemicals may be used instead, if manure is not available. Again, do this job in the early spring.

Unless new roses are purchased in containers in which they have been growing for some time, planting into side beds should be done during the winter months.

It is hardly worth raising your own roses from seed merely for patio display if space is otherwise limited. However, it is very easy to grow some roses from cuttings, notably Paul's Scarlet, the popular, old climber. It is possible to have a patio full of these red roses, all propagated from one parent in a year or two—if so desired.

Two other types of roses not already mentioned are the species grown for their fascinating red hips; and the varieties of tea roses grown as standards.

Regarding decorative rose hips, look out for *Rosa rugosa*, as the fruit is large and brightly coloured red in this species. A shrub placed at the side of a spacious terrace in a country cottage garden would be eye-catching in autumn.

Regarding standard or half standard rose trees, these can consist of hybrid tea or floribunda varieties which have been budded on to 3½ ft. (105 cm.) or 2 ft. (60 cm.) wild rose stems.

Here, I would like to draw your attention to a common mistake. The times I have seen the whole of the top part of a standard whipped off, and long wild stems left to grow from the bottom half! The supporting 3½ ft. (105 cm.) or 2 ft. (60 cm.) 'tree trunk' shouldn't be allowed to have any branches, as side stems will only produce wild roses. The spreading branches from the budded-on variety at the *top* of the 'trunk' should be lightly pruned. The new shoots from the bush at the top produce the pretty roses.

Rudbeckia are similar to single sunflowers. The variety Hurst Marmalade has vivid yellow petals and dark centres. These plants are just right for a sunny corner near the house, as they only grow to a height of around 18 in. (45 cm.)

Sow seeds during spring and transplant the young seedlings when they reach the two-leaf stage. They can go straight into patio or terrace tubs, where long-lasting flowers will appear in early autumn.

This is a good choice for those who favour the colour yellow in the garden. Young plants can follow on from a spring display of daffodils in tubs. But something else—in other tubs or pots—will be needed to provide the mid-summer colour. Consider marigolds.

Rue. Quite apart from its culinary uses, the herb *Ruta graveolens* makes an excellent patio plant —especially the variety Jackman's Blue. It grows to a height of about two feet (60 cm.), and forms a neat oval shape. The finely divided blue-grey leaves have a smell which would have to be described more as an odour than a fragrance! It knocks you back a bit if you pinch a leaf and raise it to your nose as you pass, but the smell is not much in evidence until the foliage is picked or bruised, whereas the plant is really attractive to look at even in winter, when it retains its colour.

My own specimen of Jackman's Blue rue is situated in a sunny spot by a step, and the only attention it seems to need from year to year is a quick trim after the yellow flowers fade in late summer.

Sage is another hardy evergreen herb, suitable for a sunny position at the foot of a low wall. Known botanically as *Salvia officinalis*, there is a variegated form available, which is more decorative on the patio.

The dried green leaves may be used in cooking —often served with meat dishes, but tasty also with butter and cheese on baked potatoes.

SALAD IN POTS. Here is a list of plants which we grow or have grown in pots for use in salads or sandwiches:

Tomatoes	Sweet pepper (*Capsicum*)
Cucumbers	Radishes
Lettuces	Herbs (See separate heading)
Spring onions	

And here are a few tips which I have learnt from experience:

If space is strictly limited and lettuce has to be grown in containers, choose the cos type—Little Gem is a good variety—this way the leaves can be broken off when they are only 4 in. (10 cm.) high. Leave some plants to go on growing and remove others altogether. Don't sow a whole packet at once, but just enough seeds every fortnight to give you the required number of lettuces per week—or the required number of lettuce leaves.

The same sowing plan applies to radishes—count out a small number of seeds at a time. In order to produce tender radishes, seedlings must be kept growing quickly, so give them plenty of water.

Tomatoes give good results if they are started early indoors; but don't be tempted to start too early unless you have a greenhouse as a half-way home. You won't be able to leave young plants completely unprotected outside until there is no further danger of late frosts in your district.

Sweet peppers can be planted in pots and kept in a warm room for germination in situations where a heated greenhouse is not available. But seedlings must have strong light for firm growth.

Plan to plant pepper seeds a week or two after the tomatoes, and cucumbers a week or two later, as they grow quickly.

If you hope to grow tomatoes, green peppers and cucumbers in pots out of doors, do try to obtain the special patio varieties. My own opinion is that tomatoes are the easiest plants to raise in this way—the other two usually do better in a greenhouse, unless you happen to have exactly the right kind of sheltered patio.

The success of salad crops in pots depends to a large extent on how often you water them. The compost in pots tends to dry out rather rapidly in summer. Watering *twice* a day may be necessary.

Sarcococca. There are three species of this small evergreen shrub which I can whole-heartedly recommend for the tiniest patio. Flowers appear in the midst of winter, and although not very showy, they have an extremely strong scent—branches used in cut flower displays indoors are not passed without notice. And outside it is pleasant when rich perfumes drift across paving—perhaps to be enjoyed while you are working along the borders with a trowel tidying up before spring.

The tallest of the three is the *Sarcococca hookeriana digyna* bush which grows to a height of about 3 ft. (90 cm.) and has spriggy upright branches; the leaves being 3 in. (7.5 cm.) long and narrow. White/pink flowers early in the year are followed by black berries.

S. ruscifolia is medium in height and leaf length; each leaf is 2 in. (5 cm.) long and elliptical in shape. White flowers appear early in the year and there are crimson, bead-like berries—both are seen on the bush together in some seasons. The berries are attractive to birds. The *S. humilis* bush reaches only 12 in. (30 cm.) and is the obvious choice where space is the main consideration. Oval, sharply pointed leaves are decorative all year and the little, scented, white flowers come in early spring.

Saxifraga. There are several quite distinct kinds of saxifrage suitable for different growing conditions. For example the mossy types, which are frequently seen growing in a semi-shady position in gardens, need separate treatment from the silver saxifrages which require some lime in the compost and a sunnier situation. Then there is the species which is sometimes called Mother of Thousands. It is often grown as a houseplant, but in fact it is perfectly hardy, and suited to a place on a terrace wall or rockery.

My own feeling is that the encrusted or silver saxifrages are the most suitable, as there are many species to collect, all of which form neat domes of foliage, covering pots and pans with assorted sizes of rosettes.

Among my own collection there is the tiny *Saxifraga aizoon minutifolia*, less than 2 in. (5 cm.) high with each small leaf tipped silver-white. Next in size, I have *S. cochlearis minor* and his big brother *major*; both with rosettes of strap-shaped silver-tipped leaves in neat domes. The rosettes of several other species get gradually larger in circumference, until we come to the pride of my collection, *Saxifraga* Tumbling Waters. Long, narrow, fairly stiff leaves radiate outwards from a deeply encrusted silver centre. A single, mature, rosette measures about four to five in. (10–15 cm.) across and from the middle a two-ft. (60 cm.) inflorescence arises in mid-summer. The white flowers seem to flow like a water-fall.

However, there is another silver beauty which shouldn't be missed. In some ways *S. grisebachii* is the most striking of all. It is certainly one of the earliest to flower. When the silver-dome rosette is mature, it inverts like an umbrella pushed out the wrong way. A red dot appears in the centre, and this enlarges to become a 9-in. (22.5 cm.) inflorescence. The red-tipped bracts are covered with crimson hairs, and there is a strange, heathery fragrance from the nectaries which are visible towards the top, where the red-bell flowers unfold.

Young rosettes of the silver saxifrages may be detached from the parent plants and used for propagation at almost any time except perhaps mid-winter. Choose a sandy compost. Placing white or grey stone chippings over the top of the compost, and around the base of the domes, does a lot for the final effect.

Mossy saxifrages are useful for a shady patch under a slender tree, or against a fence. In late spring, the low-growing carpet of green foliage becomes covered with delicate little, white, pink, or red cup flowers on thin stems. The species is *S. moschata;* but popular varieties include: Peter Pan—pink, and Pixie—red. Cloth of Gold is another worthwhile variety—valued for the contrasting foliage colour.

Two other saxifrages which don't fit into the above sections are mother of thousands, *S. sarmentosa*, and London pride, *S. urbicum*—a cross from *S. umbrosa*. The latter is an evergreen—good for ground-cover in the shade; pink, starry flowers are produced on inflorescence stems.

SEED LIST.

The following plants can easily be grown from seed for the patio.

Ageratum
Antirrhinum
Begonia
Coleus
Cyclamen (hardy)
Morning glory (*Ipomoea*)
Nasturtium (*Tropaeolum*)
Nicotiana
Pelargonium
Petunia
Dianthus
Impatiens
Lobelia
Marigold (*Tagetes*)
Primrose (*Primula*)
Viola

Sedum. A genus of hundreds of species of stonecrops and other plants with succulent foliage. A plant for collectors—particularly intriguing when arranged in large, flat dishes or clay pans on different levels of paving or steps. Some species are not hardy, and only suitable for out-door display during summer.

However, an interesting discovery of mine is that *Sedum praeltum*, previously grown as a greenhouse subject, is quite hardy in sheltered gardens. The emerald green colour of the spoon-shaped leaves looks fine in flower arrangements. Branches may be picked at will from plants growing in pots outside; or from specimens which may be interplanted with purple pansies.

Sedum spectabile is a fairly common plant—12 in. (30 cm.) or so high—but even this is worth considering for the pale green curls of leaves that appear early in the year; or for the pink, fluffy flowers which attract butterflies three or four at a time in late summer.

It has always been said that sedums need full sun; and indeed most of them do best in a sunny place, but I have noticed that *S. praeltum* and *S. spectabile* will grow and flower in the semi-shade.

Sempervivum. Again, there are numerous species and hybrids to collect. But you may have observed that people either become utterly fascinated by these plants, or they show no enthusiasm at all. Personally, I am attracted by the mathematical symmetry of the rosettes—I am particularly inspired by the white web of intricate lines which forms in open-weave patterns over the rosette tips of the species *Sempervivum arachnoideum* (the spider-web house leek) but the development of the small plants around the parent has also always seemed rather wonderful to me. Every species and named hybrid is distinguishable by some characteristic of its own. There are green rosettes, red rosettes, small rosettes, large rosettes; some purple-tipped; some criss-crossed with stolons; some hairy, others smooth.

Regarding the flowers, other gardeners have been known to dismiss them as not worthy of attention, whereas I consider them to be most spectacular—up they rise in the summer, strange inflorescence stems reminiscent of some science fiction story, where the author has noted the peculiar botanical features of his world. It just shows that gardening can be a matter of taste, of personal likes and dislikes, perhaps even of childhood associations.

The inflorescence stems of some varieties of the spider-web house leek really do rise to a height of more than 9 in. (22.5 cm.), although this seems impossible from such small, flat rosettes. The flowers are a subtle shade of pinky-red. (see illustration).

The interesting species in my view are the reddish hybrids of the common houseleek *S. tectorum; S. t. calcareum* with purple tips to the leaves; all the varieties of *S. arachnoideum;* the small green *S. montanum;* and *S. octopodes* like a nest of stolons. But there are others, and if you fancy these plants, you will soon find your own favourites.

Grow them in wide clay pans arranged in groups of assorted species so that the contrasting colours and sizes are displayed with maximum effect. Use John Innes compost.

Shady patio. The more gardening you have to do in a sun-less area, the more you will come to appreciate the range of possibilities. However deeply you may enjoy a sunny bed of flowers, there is certainly as much pleasure and interest to be gained from a shady bed—once you discover for yourself the large number of plants which are especially suitable for such conditions. And of course, not only just those which will grow well on the shady side of the patio or terrace, but those which you find particularly attractive.

I began my gardening in the shade with variations on *Heuchera, Hosta,* and *Hypericum.* Then I discovered the delights of *Bergenia* and *Pulmonaria.* Now, *Primula, Viola* and *Cyclamen* provide additional colour during all seasons. (See also under Patio types, and North-facing patio.)

Silene. Cultivated pink weeds—that's what some people might think of my starry flowers. Yet some species of campion are quite pretty and useful for small pots early in the year.

S. californica was collected by Dr. Worth (U.S.A.), and is recommended as one of the easiest of all annuals to grow from seed. Sow out of doors in autumn for spring flowers, and in spring for summer flowers.

Sisyrinchium is a little iris-like plant with crisp, sword-shaped leaves. *S. brachypus* grows to about 6 in. (15 cm.) high. Yellow, summer flowers open from paper-flat buds on paper-flat stems; these are quickly followed by black seed-pods. Easy to raise from seedlings.

Silver foliage plants. Besides the silver saxifrages mentioned above, other plants with silver or silver-grey leaves may be considered. For example, a medium-sized specimen of *Senecio maritima* Silver Dust looks striking in the centre of an arrangement of blue or red-flowering tub plants. Or for small patio pots, *Tanacetum densum* is just about as close in appearance to silver-white feathers as a plant could be, and the dwarf species of silver *Artemisia* has silky fine foliage.

You might decide to design yourself an unusual patio display using the silver plants suggested above in a combination with white or pink-flowering pinks. Whereas a whole garden filled with only silver plants could seem as if it lacked contrast, in the limited space of a patio, and against paving stones, silver plants can be subtly effective. (See also *Chrysanthemum*).

Stocks. If there is only a tiny, narrow space to plant flowers, sprinkle a few seeds of Virginia stock in spring for a spangly show of scented blooms four weeks later.

Dwarf double stocks look lovely outside cottage windows. Seeds of *Matthiola incana* are sown indoors in late winter and planted out in spring. Or Trysomic seven week dwarf double seed may be sown directly outside for flowers the same summer.

Where a patio is used mainly in the evenings, have a plant or two of night-scented stock in a corner close to the house. The flowers are not large or showy, but the strong scent lingers on the sultry air.

Sunny south-facing patio. A tub or two may be placed towards the front of a paved area to create bold patches of colour. A mixed planting of geraniums and petunias is hard to beat for a long-lasting bright arrangement.

A large container or bed by the house can be used to hold a climbing rose; or a ten-in. (25 cm.) clay pot will take five morning glory climbing plants, which need a trellis or wire support.

For a yellow colour-scheme choose marigolds for the tub or a large container with an orange-yellow, black-eyed-Susan vine.

In small pots and pans have *Dianthus* and other sun-loving alpines. In odd spots against low walls and between paving slabs, try the herbs with aromatic foliage such as lavender and thyme. And don't forget to plan for winter as well as summer effect. (See under Winter colour).

If you have a very sheltered sunny patio, you might like to try more exotic plants such as figs, grapes, loquats, kumquats, or passion flowers.

T

TABLE. On a patio, where there is sufficient seclusion, it is very pleasant to sit out in summer. Sometimes, a warm, sunny area out of doors—with just a little leafy shade—is a more attractive place to take a tray of tea things than a cold room indoors. And I think you will find that where there is also a table, you will be inclined to spend every possible tea-time outside.

Whether your table is a Victorian reproduction in wrought iron, a work of art in modern wood carving, or an old kitchen table with the legs sawn down, make the most of it by varnishing or painting the wood or iron-work. Black or white or natural wood-colour fit unobtrusively into the background; but green is also a satisfying colour to consider, where plants are the main feature.

Tagetes. These are the French and African marigolds. There is also a fairly new inter-specific hybrid called Afro-French i.e. a breeding between *T. erecta* (African) and *T. patula* (French).

They are all so well-known for mass-colour bedding displays, that I will only point out the fact that they are not hardy like the English marigolds; they need planting after the last frost—seeds are sown indoors and the seedlings are put outside later. But as they are fairly fast-growing, you can plant seeds quite late for summer arrangement out of doors.

It is a good idea to select the more unusual varieties. Try the single, French Cinnabar—a bright red; or Foxy, an Afro-French. Give them a sunny site; they will grow in a poor soil, if necessary.

TERRA-COTTA POTS are made in various shapes, and as a child I used to paint picture after picture of this browny-red pottery. Something about the smooth, curved sides appealed to me—and still does. I have a small collection: two hand-made in Africa with an attractive pattern round the rim; some with bulbous sides; some square; some long and narrow. At present, terra-cotta pots are inexpensive compared with other kinds of plant containers. But, unfortunately, they are becoming more and more difficult to find.

Thunbergia. The species *T. alata* is well-known as the black-eyed Susan vine. It is a useful climber for a sheltered spot against a sunny wall or fence. Sow seeds in a warm kitchen or greenhouse, later putting seedlings into a large pot or trough out of doors. Spectacular, yellow blooms with dark brown centres appear during the warm months—often lasting into the autumn.

Thyme. The old *Thymus vulgaris* is a favourite aromatic herb. It comes easily from seed. Seedlings are usually seen around the parent plants in spring. But for placing between paving stones, the variegated forms of lemon-scented *citriodorus* are more decorative. I have two beauties: Silver Queen has white margins to little leaves, and they make an attractive pattern over the plant as a whole; 'Aureus' is gold and green. There are also white and pink-flowering varieties of *Thymus serpyllum*, which are worth collecting. Choose 'Coccineus' for a particularly deep pink patch between rocks or other plants.

TRAYS. These are not essential for placing under pots outside; but in cases where drips are a nuisance, shallow trays can be found to match every size of pot.

TRELLIS. Some shrubs and climbing plants will quickly cover a wall or fence with flowers. But many need to be given support. Wire, wood or thin plastic netting can be nailed into place at the required height. Plants will then either hold on to this with their own stems or tendrils, or they can be tied in position.

TROUGHS. Long, narrow containers may be selected instead of tubs. They are especially suitable for the base of garage walls where there are no flower beds. Another idea is to have herbs in a trough under the kitchen window. Or a concrete trough may be used in the same way as a sink garden, and planted with alpines.

TUBS. A large number of plants are suitable for growing in tubs on a terrace beside steps or slopes. There are at least two advantages in growing plants in this way: choice specimens are less likely to be broken by children; and the compost can easily be made acid or alkaline. This means that you could have azaleas, camellias or rhododendrons in a sandy-peat mixture, where the surrounding garden is chalky or limy, or otherwise unsuitable.

Climbing plants can also be grown in tubs, and this is sometimes the only way of having them, when no flower beds exist at the base of house walls. Choose *Clematis*, red glory vine, honeysuckle, *Passiflora*, morning glory, or the cup-and-saucer plant.

Half-hardy summer bedding plants are particularly eye-catching in tubs. These include geraniums, petunias, fuchsias, tagetes, lobelias.

Bulbs are invaluable in the winter and spring; most are planted and put into their patio places in the early autumn. Select the choicest varieties of *Narcissus*—have them close to the house and enjoy them every time you open the door.

Tulips. Grown in tubs or giant containers, these bulbs provide welcome colour during spring. Whether you favour the dwarf species or the bigger hybrids, plant the bulbs in autumn—they may be planted a month later than *Narcissus* bulbs. Many people like to arrange them in single colour groups on their own, but they may also be mixed with plants such as wallflowers and forget-me-nots. However, it is not a good idea to plant daffodils and tulips close together, as they never do well in the same container or very small bed.

It is possible to have tulips flowering year after year from the same bulbs left in the ground—best results are gained from a warm, sunny site—but where patio plants are concerned, bulbs may be lifted after flowering and re-planted somewhere else in the garden, as the space will be needed for the summer display.

Choice depends on personal taste and available space. For a big, bold colour splash choose tall-growing Darwin tulips. Red varieties are particularly popular; but other colours include: lilac, purple, rose, orange, yellow, white. For the collector, there are many low-growing tulips available for patio planting, both natural species and hybrids, notably the various forms of *kaufmanniana* which open wide when quite close to the ground. Or another interesting species for small pans is *Tulipa greigii*. The variety Red Riding Hood has emerald green foliage marked with a brown broken-line pattern; the flowers are a vivid scarlet.

U

Umbrella palm. The newly introduced chufa is the hardy *Cyperus esculentus*, recommended both for flower arranging and for the borders of garden pools. One of its charms being that it flowers five months after the seeds are sown. Consider keeping the plant in a container to restrict the root growth. The container may be buried, leaving only the plant above soil level.

URNS. The early Florentine urns were vase-shaped with narrow necks and well-rounded middles; some were decorated on the outside with intricate mouldings. Obviously the originals are of great value for the terrace or patio. But any Ali Baba type vessel will fit splendidly into the garden scene when planted with trailing foliage. Try ivy-leaved geraniums, ivies in variety, Star of Bethlehem (white or blue-flowering), pendulous begonias and fuchsias.

V

VARIEGATED FOLIAGE plants which are suitable for use on a patio include: *Aucuba*, *Euonymus*, *Hedera*, *Hosta*, *Iris*, sage, thyme, *Veronica*. Tender plants with white or gold striped leaves may also be added during the summer months, for example: *Agave*, *Chlorophytum*, *Tradescantia*.

Veronica. There is a neat little species which grows well in pots or tidy terrace beds. It is called *V. gentianoides* and the form *variegata* with creamy-white markings on the leaves is worth finding. Racemes of pale blue flowers arise in mid-summer.

Viburnum. Several of the numerous species may be grown at the side of a large patio. Burkwoodii is a hybrid evergreen, which flowers in the spring, and *V. fragrans* or *farreri*, as it is called now, produces delicate pink flowers on bare stems in the middle of winter. Both species are scented; they will grow in almost any kind of top soil as long as they gain the sun's rays for the major part of the day. A gardening friend tells me that he thinks the finest scented *Viburnum* is undoubtedly the Korean species *V. carlesii*, which grows up to 5 ft. (150 cm.) tall after several years.

Container-grown plants may be purchased at any time, although planting out is best done in the milder period of the winter. Evergreen species may be transplanted from open ground up until late spring.

Shrubs can be propagated from cuttings or seed; but it may be five or six years before the first flowers are seen from seed.

Viola. A genus which includes the pansies and the violets in addition to the rock and alpine species. But here I will suggest only a few of my favourites among the latter. (See also the other headings).

Viola Bowles Black is a tiny dwarf annual which comes readily from seed sown at almost any time of year. Dainty in clay pans or dotted about freely in a terrace bed. Jesse East stays in bloom most of the year; and nearly everyone who sees the bonny purple and yellow flowers braving all weather asks where the plants may be obtained. Again, seeds readily germinate to provide plants at various stages of growth during the twelve months. These two varieties are excellent for placing between paving stones. In my own experience, seed sown in the autumn gives me plants that will begin to bud early in the year, whereas spring sown seed makes plants to continue the display from summer into autumn and winter.

Regarding perennial violas, several strains of *cornuta*, including Bambini, have given me hours of stimulating occupation. Some exciting results can be gained from raising your own hybrids. Seedlings do not flower the same colour as the parent, but cuttings taken from the original plants will flower the same colour as the plant from which the cutting was taken—as indeed cuttings from any plant you raise yourself will produce a specimen like the plant from which the cutting was taken. It is the seedlings that will vary. The fun comes in when you try to see just how beautiful a flower you can raise. Thereafter increasing the beauty by means of cuttings. Basal shoot cuttings root easily.

Using violas is one way of making the shady or semi-shady side of your terrace as attractive as the sunny side.

Violets. I have a white form of *V. odorata* with a green eye. But although groups of the exquisite little flowers, growing in pots or patches of shade under small shrubs, delight me every spring, they do not have the strong scent of the purple type. Queen Charlotte is a sweet-scented blue-purple variety.

Vitis. A grape vine is an unusual choice for a house wall; but where there is a south-facing aspect, it is possible to have, not only an interesting leafy pattern all summer, but the hope of fruit in the autumn.

Seeds taken from grape pips have germinated and quickly grown into small climbing plants for me; but if you intend to eat your own fruit, or make your own wine, it is advisable to purchase young plants of a named variety which has been especially selected for its habit of developing and fruiting early when raised out of doors. Try Villard, a white-grape variety, or Chambourcin (black), or Riesling Sylvaner (browny-yellow).

The flowers will appear in late spring out of doors, and the fruit should ripen in autumn.

Rotten manure is almost a necessity in growing grapes. A mixture of three parts of loam to one part of well-rotted manure suits them. Remember to top-dress the soil with further supplies of rich, manure-compost every year.

W

Walls. There is probably a walled garden in every gardener's dreams. Walls give protection to plants and seclusion for people. At least there is usually one wall on every patio and that is the house wall.

An historic cottage not far from where I live has climbing plants and shrubs on the front walls, and looks as pretty as a post-card all the year. In the late winter, one half of the cottage is covered with yellow jasmine flowers, reaching to the eaves; in the spring there are white flowers on a *Pyracantha* around a window; in summer, pink roses meet over the top of the porch; in autumn, Virginia creeper lights up the other half of the house with orange leaves, and red berries follow on the *Pyracantha*.

These plants are all exposed to winds and rain, although the cottage has a south-west facing aspect. The arrangement of plants is well worth considering for an east- or west-facing wall too; and the winter jasmine will grow even on a north wall.

Another kind of wall is made only two or three feet high—an open topped plant wall. If you are building one yourself, remember to place plenty of rubble at the base for drainage. And every three feet along the centre, construct a partition of bricks. This should not be visible from the top—it is to give the wall strength. A layer of compost goes over the rubble and partition bricks.

Yet another wall is the one standing away from the house, perhaps as a side wall to the garden, or a garage wall, or an out-building surrounded by paving.

It is here, in a really sunny, sheltered position, that you might like to try peaches, nectarines, loquats or figs. These plants can be grown in large containers or tubs; and there are several interesting points about their cultivation.

Regarding peaches, it is possible to grow plants from seed and obtain good fruit. Several of my friends have tried this and produced satisfying results. It has been found that protecting plants from extreme wet conditions in the winter with some sort of shelter above is beneficial. Peach trees flower early, so the same rough shelter could become a shield against slight frost, and artificial pollination is essential to ensure a record crop.

If you wish to purchase young plants, the varieties Rochester and Peregrine are suitable for growing out of doors. If you wish to try raising your own plants from stones taken from eating fruit, set the seed in a small pot at first, keeping the pot on a window sill in a cool room.

It should be noted that nectarines are less hardy in the open than peaches.

But loquats—which belong to the same *Rosaceae* family as the peaches, and also originate from China—make an excellent choice for patio tubs. The foliage is splendid—enormous leaves, which are covered with downy hairs at first, turn glossy as they grow—and white, scented flowers form early in the year followed by small fruits like pear-shaped peaches. It has to be admitted that fruit will not form unless the plant has the right kind of sheltered environment. However, it is hardy in most districts, and worth keeping for its one foot long, evergreen leaves. These come through the winter, providing the compost is kept on the dry side during the coldest months. This usually involves some sort of over-head structure.

Remember that plants in tubs require regular watering in summer; they also need mulching with rotted manure every spring. It is rewarding giving plants a simple programme of attention, as there is a thrill to be gained from seeing your own peach tree laden with golden fruit. Friends will probably say they didn't know it was possible in a cool climate.

Wallflowers. Not surprisingly they grow well in between bricks, and they are a good choice for open-topped walls—lovely with forget-me-nots on the ground beneath. One of my earliest memories is the sight of wallflowers growing wild down a cliff-face. They are extremely hardy plants which cling to tiny cracks of soil with tenacity—standing up to icy blasts of wind and rain. Yet they still become a blaze of colour with their richly scented flowers bursting out from black buds.

To raise young plants for the patio, sow seeds in early summer. They can be transplanted a few inches apart in some other area of the garden. In autumn, the maturing plants are placed in tubs, or beds, for winter greenery and spring flowers. It may interest you to know that if for any reason your seeds are sown late and your plants don't make it to flowering size the first season, they may be kept over for another year, when they will make bigger plants.

Blood Red is my favourite, but Ruby Gem is another deep red, or you may prefer the yellow Cloth of Gold. Gardeners who like pastel colours will enjoy Fair Lady Mixed. Botanists and/or geologists may go for the little Siberian wallflower, *Cheiranthus allionii*. But apparently this plant is now an *Erysimum*.

West-facing patio. Camellias are suitable for this position. They are often recommended for the north-facing aspect, but mine seem to do better against the house in a west-facing position. There is a fragrant, white, summer-flowering jasmine to one side and tiny purple violas underneath the camellia.

Try also a flax, *Linum narbonense* with grey-green foliage and rich blue flowers. Or if your sunny patio has a corner shaded by a fence for part of the day, this is the place where fuchsias and busy Lizzies will do well. They may be grown in tubs or large containers of any kind.

In raised beds, you could have a selection of some of the half-hardy annuals, such plants as dwarf asters, nemesia, tagetes and zinnia.

The sunniest pots or urns can be filled with geraniums, petunias and lobelias for bright blobs of colour against plain paving stones. (See also Climbing plants).

White flowers grouped in pots, tubs, window boxes, hanging baskets and raised patio beds can result in a strange effect somewhere between simplicity and sophistication. I have decided recently, that one bold arrangement per season is the most satifying way of using white flowers *en masse* out of doors.

In spring, my choice might be white daffodils or white hyacinths—perhaps with white violets (but here again I am revising my views, white violets look lovely growing semi-wild underneath shrubs). In summer, maybe I would choose white geraniums with white star of Bethlehem trailing over the side of the pot. Or for semi-shade in summer, I would select from white fuchsias, begonias, and busy Lizzies; foxgloves for shade—they flower even against a north-facing wall. In winter, a patch of white *Cyclamen neapolitanum* is a near-perfect choice.

Window boxes. Besides the familiar spring, summer, autumn and winter displays, consider the desirability of the all-the-year box.

The usual method is to change the plants in autumn for the winter and spring show, say, bulbs, primroses, primulas, forget-me-nots or *Bellis* daisies; and again in late spring for half-hardy summer bedding plants, which have been raised elsewhere. But other methods include: a permanent planting of hardy cyclamen; dwarf conifers and/or other shrubs; a collection of herbs or alpines.

However you plan your box, the best results are bound to depend on frequent watering in summer during dry weather periods. And don't forget to renew the compost, or where a permanent scheme is preferred, give some fertilizer from time to time. Conifers need a peaty compost; cyclamen respond to a top-dressing of leaf-mould, bonfire ash and bonemeal; and alpines are improved by stone chippings spread around the roots.

Although neutral colours are chosen for window boxes for obvious reasons—they shouldn't clash or distract from the flowers—a yellow box with yellow daffodils matching a yellow front door was seen this year. In the shade selected by the owner, it was quite striking.

WINTER PATIO. If gardening during the cold months is not one of your favourite occupations, and you are only interested in having a gay show of flowers while you are sitting out during the summer, there is something to be said for clean, wind-swept paving with, perhaps, just a few brown leaves blowing about. Or you might fancy a stone statue staring into space, or a lonely urn to form a focal point in an otherwise empty area.

But a popular idea now is to plan for the winter effect all the year. This is done by choosing evergreens, and plants with interesting stems and general outlines, so that they look good even when devoid of leaves. In summer the scene is brightened with a tub or two of colourful annuals or half-hardy red or blue-flowering plants.

One of the best winter displays I have seen in an otherwise paved garden, consisted of a curved, raised bed filled with clean compost and well-spaced heathers; *Thuya occidentalis* Holmstrupensis, a pointed green conifer; *Juniperus chinensis* Pyramidalis, dull green; *Thuya rheingold*, a bright, golden conifer; *Hebe elliptica; Hebe* Autumn Glory; *Lavandula* Hidcote, and a group of species tulips.

A camellia makes a splendid subject for a giant container. Camellias are perfectly hardy, and the glossy, dark green leaves will not lose their lustre, so long as the roots are given an acid, peaty compost, which is not allowed to go dry. They used to be considered tender plants, due to the fact that the flowers, which come early in the year, must not catch the morning sun after a frosty night. But this little difficulty can be overcome by placing the pot in a north or west-facing position.

Other plants for the winter garden include:

Aucuba	—variegated foliage.
Bergenia	—large leaves; pink flowers.
Calluna	—yellow foliage effect.
Crocus	—
Cyclamen	—Silver-marked foliage and flowers.
Dianthus	—grey foliage.
Erica	—red, green or yellow effect from flowers or foliage.
Euonymus	—variegated leaves.
Hypericum	—ground cover.
Iris	—several species for winter foliage or winter flowers.
Ivy	—trailing or climbing.
Kerria	—green stems.
Lavender	—grey foliage.
Narcissus	—
Pulmonaria	—spotted leaves; pink and blue flowers early March.
Sage	—
Saxifrage	—silver encrusted rosettes.
Sempervivum	—silver-white cushions.
Thyme	—
Violas	—
Wallflowers	—

(See also under Climbing plants).

Wistaria sinensis. Some gardeners consider this to be the most beautiful climbing plant for a house wall. Long racemes of pale purple flowers hang downwards from the stems in mid-summer.

Propagation of an established specimen consists of pegging down a side stem during late spring. The part of the stem under the ground should root within a year. This process can be helped by making a shallow cut into the stem where it is to go underground. Support the top half of the stem as it emerges from the ground again. It may be tied to a cane.

To prune an old plant, cut back the stems to just above three healthy buds in late winter. Give plants a south or west-facing wall.

Z

Zebrina pendula. A useful little silver and

purple-striped trailer for summer hanging baskets.

Zinnia hybrids are flower arrangers' specials —probably because they last well in water when picked. The favourite seems to be the green variety Envy. But for pots on paving, you might like to sow a few seeds of the brightly coloured, mixed varieties. Colours include: pink, orange, red, white, and yellow. Sow the seed indoors early in the year, and transplant the young seedlings into their patio positions in late spring. Choose a sunny place.

Zygocactus truncatus. The well-known Christmas cactus has recently been re-classified as a *Schlumbergera;* but most people still think of it as a *Zygocactus*. By any name, it makes an easy-to-grow 'leafy' plant for pots or hanging baskets out of doors in summer. Give it a peaty compost, and keep dry for the last month of summer; by autumn, the flower buds will begin to form in the areoles at the tips of the leaf-stems. Take it indoors as a flowering house plant for the winter.

Gardening can be satisfying in many ways. I will end with a line from Coleridge. It is taken from a description of himself written in 1796: 'All else is *blank;* but I *will* be (please God) an horticulturalist and a farmer.'

It may be difficult to be a farmer on a patio, but it is possible to be an horticulturalist in the smallest space!

LIST OF ADDRESSES

SOCIETIES

Alpine Garden Society: 58 Denison House, 296 Vauxhall Bridge Rd., London SW1.
Nat. Begonia Soc., 50 Woodlands Farm Rd., Erdington, Birmingham B24 0PG.
Nat. Cactus & Succulent Soc., 19 Crabtree Rd., Botley, Oxford.
Brit. Nat. Carnation Soc., 1 Woodham Rd., Catford, London SE6.
Nat. Dahlia Soc., 26 Burns Rd., Leamington Spa, Warwickshire.
Brit. Fuchsia Soc., 72 Ash Lane, Hale, Altrincham, Cheshire.
Brit. Iris Soc., 72 South Hill Park, London NW3 2SN.
Brit. Pansy and Viola Soc., 43 Northfield Lane, Horbury, Wakefield, Yorks.
Brit. Pelargonium and Geranium Soc., 129 Aylesford Ave., Beckenham, Kent.
Brit. Pteridological Soc. (Ferns), 46 Sedley Rise, Loughton, Essex.
Heather Soc. Yew Trees, Horley Rd., Horley, Surrey.
Internat. Camellia Soc., Bodnant Gardens, Tal-y-Cafn, Denbighshire.
Orchid Soc. of Great Brit., 87 Brookman's Ave., Brookman's Park, Herts.
Royal Nat. Rose Soc., Chiswell Green Lane, St. Albans, Herts.
Saintpaulia and Houseplant Soc., 82 Rossmore Court, Park Rd., London NW1.
The Royal Horticultural Society, Vincent Sq., London SW1P 2PE.

Garden Design and Construction: George G. Whitelegg Ltd., Knockholt, Nr. Sevenoaks, Kent.
The Patio Scene: J. Newall Ltd., 171 Lavender Hill, London SW11.
Stone Art: Haylands, Kimblewick Rd., Great Kimble, Aylesbury, Bucks. (Garden tables, benches, fountains, containers, ash-trays).
Q-Cloche, Willowbank Wharf, Ranelagh Gardens, Putney Bridge, London S.W.6. (Clay pots & pans [many shapes] and patio frames).
Keramikos Pottery: 5 St. Mary's Road, Longfleet, Poole, Dorset. (Bonsai containers).

NURSERIES

T. A. Bennett (Monica Bennett), Cypress Nursery, Powke Lane, Blackheath, Birmingham. (Pelargoniums).
Bressingham Gardens, Diss, Norfolk. (Unusual outdoor plants: mail order).
Broadleigh Gardens, Barr House, Bishops Hull, Taunton, Somerset. (Miniature bulbs).
Thomas Butcher, Wickham Rd., Shirley, Croydon, Surrey. (Greenhouse plants and ferns).
Hillier & Sons, Winchester, Hants. (Trees and shrubs).
Holly Gate Nurseries, Spear Hill, Ashington, Surrey. (Cacti & Succulents).
M. Holtzhausen, 14 High Cross St., St. Austell, Cornwall. (Rare bulbs).
Hortico Ltd., Spalding, Lincs. (General bulbs).
Hurst, Witham, Essex. (Garden seeds).
W.E.Th. Ingwersen, Birch Farm Nursery, Gravetye, E. Grinstead, Sussex. (Alpine plants, sink gardens).
J. A. Mars of Haslemere, Surrey GU27 3DW. (Hardy Cyclamen & Hardy Orchids).
McBean's Orchids, Cooksbridge, Lewes, Sussex.
Perry's Hardy Plant Farm, Enfield, Mddx. (Water plants).
Reginald Kaye, Waitham Nurseries, Siverdale, Carnforth, Lancs. (Alpines and ferns).
T. Rochford, Turnford Hall, Broxbourne, Herts. (Houseplants).
Thompson & Morgan, London Rd., Ipswich, Suffolk. (Largest selection of seeds).
Wyck Hill Geraniums, Stow-on-the-Wold, Glos.

AMERICAN ADDRESSES

SOCIETIES

American Begonia Soc., 1510 Kimberley Ave., Anaheim, Calif. 92802.
American Orchid Soc., Botanical Museum of Harvard University, Cambridge, Mass. 02138.
The Bromeliad Soc., 1811 Edgecliff Drive, Los Angeles, Calif.
The Saintpaulia International Soc. P.O. Box 10604, Knoxville, Tenn. 37919.

NURSERIES

Alberts & Merkel Bros., P.O. Box 537, Boynton Beach, Fla. 33435 (Orchids).
Alexander Heimlich, 71 Burlington St., Woburn, Mass. (Bulbs).
Burgess Seed & Plant Co., 67 E. Battle Creek St., Galesburg, Mich. 49053. (Houseplants).
Hausermans Orchids, Box 363, Elmhurst, Ill.

Henriettas Nursery, 1345 N. Brawley, Fresno, Calif. 93705 (Cactus).
Margaret Ilgenfritz, Box 665, Monroe, Mich. 48161. (Orchids).
Merry Gardens, Camden, Maine, 04843. (House-plants).
Wilson Bros., Roachdale, Ind. 46172. (Pelargoniums).
Siskiyou Rare Plant Nursery, 522 Franquette St., Medford, Oregon, USA. (Rock plants).
Van Ness Water Gardens, 2460 N. Euclid Ave., Upland, Calif. (Water plants).

INDEX